Nobody Will Believe You

A young girl
abused by her stepfather.
A true story of unbreakable courage.

MARY MANNING

WITH NICOLA PIERCE

THE O'BRIEN PRESS
DUBLIN

First published 2015 by The O'Brien Press Ltd,
12 Terenure Road East, Rathgar, Dublin 6, Ireland.
Tel: +353 1 4923333; Fax: +353 1 4922777
E-mail: books@obrien.ie
Website: www.obrien.ie

ISBN: 978-1-84717-668-4

1 3 5 7 9 10 8 6 4 2
15 17 19 18 16

Publisher's Note:
In publishing Mary Manning's courageous and important story, we reviewed
numerous documents proving, convincingly, the truth of what Mary has
suffered. The Health Board document at the end of the book is merely one
of many in our possession from legal and court sources, social and health
authorities, and other sources.

Michael O'Brien, Publisher

Cover images:
Front cover photography © Alamy (Posed by model)
Back cover photography: author's own
Cover design: Two Associates

Printed and bound by Nørhaven, Denmark.
The paper in this book is produced using pulp from managed forests.

Dedication

To Karl who journeyed to the darkest pools of my soul to plant the seeds of love, and to each of my children, whose strength of spirit gave me the courage to carry on.

Acknowledgements

To my two brothers, for standing with me.

To Andrew, for always being in my thoughts.

A big 'thank you' also to: Ronan, Jill, Judith, Ann, Jamie, Norma, Ben, Clint, Stevie, Jimmy, Mick and Liam. Thank you to Nicola for the support, endless phone calls and for bringing it all together.

There are many others along the way who have lighted my path and held my hand at different times: Sean Moncrieff and all at *The Sean Moncrieff Show* on Newstalk, especially Claire; Michael O'Brien and all the staff at The O'Brien Press, with a special thank you to Helen.

What a huge journey we've taken together!

And finally

To Dad and Grand Ma.

I'm over half-way through writing this book. Maybe I'm even further along than that, but it has suddenly become too hard again. I'm emotional and keep breaking down. Perhaps the reality is settling in regarding what's going to happen – that these writings are going to be, in a few short months, an actual book that will sit on the shelves in bookshops and libraries for anyone to pick up and flick through, anyone at all.

I'm afraid of how I'll be judged. I have this acute fear that people I'll never meet will think I could have done more. They might think I could have found some way of stopping that rapist all those years ago. The shame is as real today on this dismal November afternoon as it was when I was a young girl.

And there's another side to what I'm feeling – guilt. I feel like I'm betraying *him* with the book. I see his face at night, I hear his voice in my head and I could swear that his spirit is all around me. Is he hurt, angry or is he championing me to continue with the story, in the hope that I'll finally be different in some way?

PROLOGUE

My love of shoes probably stemmed from my mother's large, lovely and expensive collection. There was one pair in particular that I cherished; they were silver with a low heel and glistened like diamonds in the sun. It became a habit of mine to sneak into her room to try on those shoes over and over again, each time hoping that perhaps this time they might fit. However, they were always too big for me.

Around ten years ago I found this designer, whose shoes – glorious shoes – are sold in boutiques around the country. Today I have my own large, lovely and expensive collection. They are works of art, in a variety of clashing colours and wild patterns. In some cases the patterns spread all over the sole, which makes it seem like an appalling idea to actually walk about in them. And, to be honest, they are not the most comfortable to wear, so I would advise against wearing them to go shopping or anything else that involves a lot of walking.

But, my goodness, are these shoes gorgeous! They quickly became my new reason to go shopping. There is a website, but I am not handy with computers, which is undoubtedly a good thing. I would hate to think of the money I might spend if shopping for my favourite thing merely involved a few clicks of the mouse.

My shoes mean a lot to me. I feel good when I wear them. Actually, I don't just feel good, I feel strong. It might sound a little strange, but the truth is that when I put on a pair of uncomfortable, wacky, loud shoes with tottering high heels, they help me to feel grounded, which is why I chose to wear my favourite pair to Sean's funeral.

Sean is – or was – my stepfather. He married my mother when I was ten years old.

The shoes I wore to his funeral are covered in bunny rabbits. Not that you would be able to see them if you weren't standing right next to me, and staring at my feet. Really, only I'd know that they were plastered in multiple bunny rabbits and black stars. I suppose I could describe them as similar in shape to Victorian booties. Does that make sense? They have to be laced up, though there are only five holes, and the laces are made of the same material as the shoes. However, I didn't wear them that day for the bunnies. I wore them because the shoes are framed in a vibrant pink and – for me – pink represents love. Choosing to wear those particular shoes was me taking steps, if you like, to protect myself.

Funerals are never easy for anyone.

Those shoes kept me true to myself. I was not going to apologise for anything, but neither did I mean to cause any harm. Pink is love and I wanted to – needed to – feel love that day for everyone present, but most of all for myself.

I wore my long black coat, which allowed my shoes to properly shine, and provided another layer of protection and self-preservation. We wear coats to shield us from cold and wet weather; that morning I used mine to shield myself from casual onlookers and, yes, Sean's siblings and their families. I was unsure of the reception I'd receive. To top off the coat and shoes, there was a small angel in my pocket. I wasn't taking any chances. It was silver with a tiny dot of purple amethyst in the centre. I asked the angel to protect me and *my* family. Every now and then I discreetly stuck my hand into my pocket to touch it as the priest spoke on and on.

I wanted to look well. What woman doesn't?, but it went deeper than that. What I mean is that I didn't want to betray myself, to show my inner scars. I wanted to look well and not like a victim. And certainly, not like a woman who had been raped repeatedly for over ten years by this man who was now dead; this man, my stepfather, who was also the father of five of my children.

CHAPTER ONE

The year was 1972 and life was good, really good. Not that I appreciated that at the time; hindsight is a wonderful thing. In any case I was just a little girl whose only hardship was the silly white miniskirt I had to wear to tennis lessons every Saturday morning.

We, that is my parents, Rikki, my younger brother, and I, lived in a mobile home. This was just temporary, however. Dad, who was a mechanic by trade, ran a busy garage and shop, selling petrol and fixing cars, on the Drogheda Road in Ardee. His father, my grandfather Paul, had given him a large plot of land for the business, and this allowed Dad to start building our new house right next to it. My parents worked long hours and Dad even planned to open a small restaurant on the site.

It's a long time ago or maybe so much has happened since that it is hard to remember specific details. I have to prod my memory into action and hope for the best. After a while I can see the builders, in my mind, making our house grow out of the ground, brick by brick. Dad, wearing his old beret cap, is supervising the build from the roof of the garage. I call up to him; he smiles, but tells me to go away for fear of something falling down on top of me. In case he has hurt my feelings he smiles again.

My brother and I spent a lot of time with our paternal grandparents while the house was being built. They lived down the street from us – well, down the street and up a lane, in a cottage made up of just four rooms. The most commonly used was the kitchen-cum-dining room. I particularly loved my grandmother's back garden because it was like entering some kind of wild, magical jungle. Grandma understood the power of plants – their healing powers. Where I saw clumps of green and weeds on our walks together, she would see medicine.

We would frequently go out walking together and as we walked she constantly scanned the bog and surrounding area. It was almost like going shopping with her. One minute we would be chatting away about school or something like that, when she'd suddenly shriek in delight and surge forward, pulling a plastic bag from the pocket of her Sunday coat as I did my best to work out the source of her excitement. I marvelled at her hunched over an ordinary looking shrub, carefully taking only what she needed.

When I asked why she wouldn't take more, since it was free and nobody owned it, she explained that she was making sure that the plant would continue to thrive so that it would be there the next time we passed it.

One time we stopped at this rose-hip bush for what seemed like hours, but was probably only twenty minutes or so. Carefully, she gathered enough for the two of us as she liked to make rosehip syrup and, just as carefully, she left enough for the birds or whoever else might want some. Checking she had left enough, she said, 'Nature provides enough for everyone and everything as long as we aren't greedy.'

Of course we had to be careful with the bog. Wellington boots were absolutely necessary for these excursions and we did our best to avoid holes and soft, wet patches that may want to hold onto our boots. It fascinated me. How many times did Grandma have to pull me out of soft mud and then return to do battle for my boot? She never seemed to mind the amount of times I got stuck. It was slightly unnerving and I would find myself fretting that maybe I would be sucked into the ground. Yet I always felt safe when I was beside her and she always, always managed to retrieve my boot. As cars raced by us, she would shake her head and sigh over the fact that the drivers probably knew nothing of the wondrous bounty that was just a few yards from the road.

Her shed was her private studio. There were rows of old jamjars filled with a variety of nature: dried plants, slow vines, gooseberries, raspberries and plenty of stuff I didn't recognise. Herbs were hung from the roof to dry them out, before being stored carefully in the jars with their names on the labels. Her garden was, to my naive eyes, an unruly mess. Wild and vibrantly coloured flowers flared throughout, along with prickly thistles and dock leaves. Nevertheless she knew the whereabouts and identity of every little thing that grew there and loved to take me for a tour, pointing out the different plants and their properties to me. If I looked distracted, she would have me touch the leaf or stem, repeat its name and smell it. I understand now that she was hoping to pass on her knowledge to me. 'See that there!' she would say. I dutifully glanced over as she described the benefits of the plant once it was boiled and added to another one that looked the exact same to me. I saw weeds, while she saw something more precious than gold dust.

Even today, when I spy lavender growing in my own garden or smell it, I am instantly transported back to my grandmother's house: it's the smell that

I most associate with her. Her plants cured a list of ailments from colds to mysterious rashes, as well as ugly red spots and stubborn warts. I imagine it was therapeutic work, collecting and drying out plants, labelling jam jars and knowing exactly what to do with them. Unfortunately my grandmother did not allow herself to enjoy it too much. In fact she suffered from a relentless guilt that she was, in some way, doing something that the church might frown upon. To combat any potential evil she might be party to, she attended mass not just daily, but twice a day, in the morning and again in the evening. I think she felt that mass would purge her of any sins she might be innocently committing in the shed.

She had a genuine love for nature. One time she told me rather excitedly that she had something wonderful to show me. Goodness knows what I expected to see. She led me down the path to a pile of brown leaves. Pushing these aside, her big moment, she stood back and waited for my response. It was a tiny thing in the ground with two skinny shoots sprouting from it. 'It's a chestnut tree!' she announced breathlessly. I didn't know what she wanted me to say or do so I just imitated her excitement. She seemed to regard it as a reward for the year's work she had put into the garden.

Not surprisingly, Grandma wasn't one for dressing up. For mass she might quickly dab on some old lipstick and then throw on her best hat and coat over the worn dress and tights that were always grubby from the garden. On Sundays, when my parents were working in the shop, she called for Rikki and me and took us to church. Mass was so boring, but I enjoyed the long way back to Grandma's cottage afterwards where we would find my grandfather in his usual spot, sitting at the kitchen table and engrossed in the Sunday newspaper.

He was a stern-looking man, but I knew he was fond of me. I'd make a bee-line for him and he would ask me about mass and what I had learnt that day. Not having paid much attention to the gospel, I was obliged to concoct one of my own with the moral intact. In spite of his grumpy nature he would smile at my attempts to regale him with that morning's lesson. As young as I was, I could see right through his grumpiness. He pretended not to be paying me much attention, pretended that the newspaper was absorbing all his interest, but I would see him watching my every move and the smile that tried not to break through. When I had drained the morning mass of all entertainment he would ask me about school. I always made sure I had something for him. One Sunday morning I proudly recited my latest academic accomplishment, the two-times table, blissfully unaware of numerous mistakes, and enjoyed his eruption into laughter.

My grandparents had little in common. Auld Paul, as we called him, enjoyed his drink and sometimes kept irregular hours, not coming home until the small hours of the morning. When she was annoyed with him – *really* annoyed with him – Grandma would retreat to her garden and sit under the tree. She once told me that when he was younger, Auld Paul was known in the town for lighting his cigarettes with five-pound notes. She said, 'He had money to burn in the pub, but I wouldn't have a loaf of bread on the table!'

The only thing that I didn't enjoy about the visit was Grandma's home-made chicken soup. I still remember the smell today. Hours and hours went into the boiling of the bones and chicken bits, including the neck. She ladled it out into my bowl and I would feel nauseous at the sight of the beige liquid, with little lumps of meat that was topped off with ugly pools of grease. Every week I looked into the pot hoping to see an improved version of it, but it was always the same. I tried to work out a way of emptying the bowl without touching a drop. Briefly I considered throwing it into her big kitchen range, but it would put out the fire and I knew if I were to accidentally spill it onto the floor my bowl would be immediately refilled from that massive pot that never seemed to run dry. There were two rewards for us on finishing the soup. One was monetary: Auld Paul knew I hated the thing and would promise me a shiny ten-pence coin if I ate my share and the second was Grandma's champ. Now, this I loved. Her potatoes were perfectly mashed up, just the way I liked them, with slivers of onion and plenty of butter and milk. It was a difficult task, to get through that soup, but I wanted the champ and I needed that coin. Ironically enough, my brother and I used our hard-won prize money to buy sweets to get rid of the taste of the soup. However, there was worse soup to come, one that was snotty green and watery in texture. Not surprisingly, Rikki and I hated it on sight, but we forced it into us for her sake. Much later we discovered that the chief ingredient was nettles from the garden. Nettles, my grandmother believed, would give a person good health and a long life.

Some days I literally had to sing for my food. I was in the school choir and Grandma often begged me to perform her favourite hymn, 'Morning Has Broken'. I was never too sure if I was a good singer, despite the fact I could hit the high notes alright, but she would assure me, week after week, that I had a beautiful voice.

Grandma also introduced me to the historic sites in the area. Every couple of months we went to look at the 'Jumping Church'. This famous landmark was a constant source of disappointment to me because I never saw it jump, not even once. Legend has it that an evil man was buried in the church's graveyard and, being consecrated ground, the church wanted rid of his body so the boundary wall jumped inwards, thereby excluding him from its sacred territory. I found it unimpressive in every way, seeing how all that was left of the church was one wall and a mess of stones. Why was it even called a church now, let alone a jumping one? As we walked away from the ruin I would continually glance back, hoping to see some movement, but I never did. Maybe my grandmother was also hoping to see it jump and that's why we visited it so often.

My other grandmother lived just outside the town. She had a big garden that was always perfectly neat with not a blade of grass out of place. Everything had its proper place and that was that. She wasn't as warm as Grandma. In fact I would say that my mother only got close to her mother in her later years, who had always struck me as an stern woman. My grandfather was a small, quiet man. It was a large, extended family, but I never felt that there was a closeness or bond between my mother's family, though perhaps I am getting mixed up with what happened later on.

CHAPTER TWO

Before they got married, Mother worked in the post office. Perhaps that's where he met her or maybe it was a local dance. I'm not entirely sure. What I do know, however, is that when they stood at the altar in 1963, I was already on the way. I have some photographs of the big day and they both look genuinely happy as they smile and laugh into the camera. Later on, my mother would say she only married him because she was pregnant. That explains a lot.

By the time I arrived they were over in the UK, living beside Dad's sister in Dorset. We didn't stay long. Eighteen months after I was born, we were back in Ardee for the birth of my brother Rikki.

It never occurred to me that we were well off. At that time, in the mid-sixties, most people could not afford a car while my mother had her own. Rikki and I had tennis lessons, piano lessons and Irish dancing classes and no doubt assumed that this was normal for other children too. Because of what happened in the not too distant future I do struggle to remember the little, ordinary details that are part and parcel of any childhood. Fortunately there are some remnants still floating around in my mind. For instance, my mother enjoyed watching *The Late Late Show* and David Attenborough's nature programmes. The music that I grew up listening to was Neil Diamond, Willie Nelson and Kris Kristofferson. In my grandparents' house we watched *Some Mothers Do 'Ave 'Em*. And like any Irish family we went to mass every Sunday.

My mother was quite a glamorous woman and liked to look well. At some point she even did some modelling. In her spare time she was a wonderful cook who gave us the most delicious meals. Dad was the successful businessman around town who wanted to expand the petrol station and open a restaurant. They were both outgoing with the customers and worked long hours. Their social life was largely built around the golf club where they would meet the other successful business people in the town. There were plenty of weekends away with the golf club to places around Ireland, England and even Spain. Alcohol was a normal part of everyday life, from gin and tonics at lunch to dinner dances, parties and Christmas balls.

I don't remember any rows or feeling that either of them was unhappy with their lot. They both focussed on building up the business and made sure Rikki and I didn't want for anything.

The most frequent visitor to our home was Mother's aunt May, who was her father's sister. I never really liked this woman. Broad and tall in stature, with blonde, wavy hair, it seemed to me that she sort of took over whenever she came around. I felt she dominated my mother. During her visits Rikki and I had to leave the room. Mother just wasn't available to us when May was over. May couldn't drive so would request to be brought places, dropped off, collected and be driven home again. At some point she had a beau. They wrote to each other for years, but never married. I don't know why.

May lived about four miles outside town, in a semi-detached cottage. It was on the main road – or what used to be the main road – from Ardee to Stabannon. We didn't visit her much. From what I remember her house was neither particularly neat nor clean. Plus it had a strange musty smell and the air felt almost chilly. Out the back she had a large garden of two to three acres. How Grandma would have loved it. May, however, was not into planting herbs or plants; grass was the only thing growing there. Years later, after her death, when I was helping to pack up her house, we found sacks upon sacks of empty gin and whiskey bottles out the back.

The new house wasn't entirely finished when we moved into it, which was around the end of July in 1973. The reason we moved in early was that our caravan had burnt to the ground. The reason the caravan burned to the ground was that Rikki and I were in it one day, alone, sitting in front of the coal fire, or maybe it was a gas fire. It seems peculiar today that there was a fire at all in a caravan. He was six years old at the time while I was almost eight, and he was in a giddy mood. He had the little sweeping brush in his hand and kept telling me he was going to set it on fire. I was telling him not to. However, he jabbed the brush into the flames and, sure enough, it went on fire. He hadn't actually meant this to happen and panicked, throwing the brush under the curtains, perhaps believing this would make the brush disappear. Of course it was only a matter of seconds before the curtains were set alight, along with everything else. Dad burst in the door and picked up the both of us, took us out, and set us down before racing back in to rescue some important documents.

When he came back out to where we were, he collapsed. My mother was working in the petrol station, some hundred yards away. She must have come running, but I don't remember seeing anyone in particular. There was a lot of screaming and shouting. People suddenly appeared – lots of them – like a noisy swarm of bees. There was plenty of running back and forth, pushing and shoving. Buckets of water were fetched and a line was hastily formed as a battle commenced with the blazing caravan. As I sit here, writing this, I can see those flames bellowing high into the sky. The heat was tremendous. Someone called the fire brigade and the ambulance. They weren't long in coming. The fire brigade put out the fire while the ambulance men tended to my father. Rikki and I were pushed aside and we couldn't really see what was happening. At some point my grandmother arrived to take us back with her. Next thing we knew was that Dad was put on a stretcher. My mother climbed into the back of the ambulance. I wanted to go with her, but wasn't allowed. Someone, maybe Grandma, pulled me away from the doors as they were closed. He was rushed to Our Lady of Lourdes Hospital in Drogheda.

My memories begin to blur here. I was probably traumatised, as I can't believe how little I remember of that day.

Routine tests uncovered the fact that Dad had cancer. I know he came home briefly after this discovery, but I just don't remember him in the new house. They took him back in to operate, but when they opened him up, he was 'riddled', beyond help. All Rikki and I knew was that about a month or so after the fire we returned home from school, one afternoon, to find May sitting at the kitchen table. I tensed immediately. There was something about the expression on her face or the fact that she seemed to be waiting for us. Well, we weren't left wondering for long. Without any attempt to prepare us in any way, May blurted out, 'Your father is dead!' It was the 26 September 1973, the day that my childhood died.

Of course May had little experience of breaking horrific news to young children, but today I wonder why Mother or Grandma didn't tell us. My dislike of May has probably a lot to do with the shortness and awfulness of those four words. Rightly or wrongly, I found it impossible to like her after she told me that Dad was dead, as if the child that I was blamed her in some way for it.

The funeral was one of the biggest ever seen in Ardee. The fact that Dad was so young, came from such a well-known family and was one of the most successful businessmen in the town brought people out in their hundreds. The mass took place in Ardee church and he was buried in Ballapousta graveyard. I don't remember much about it. Mother wore a black dress and a large black hat which had netting over the front of it that covered her face, but she wore lots of hats, and turbans, so that didn't really strike me as being odd. I remember being upset in the mortuary. It was just my mother, Rikki and me. The others had headed off to the church. I knew Dad was in the coffin, but I was too small to see him and because of that I had my doubts that he was dead at all. Surely he was just asleep and would wake up before they put the lid on the coffin. Then Mother lifted me up so that I could give him a kiss goodbye. He looked so strange. Was this really him? I was still upset, but gave him a kiss on his cheek. It was icy cold. I hadn't expected that.

It amazes me today that my memory of this huge event is so vague. However, my emotions are as strong as ever: such grief and sadness that has not dimmed over the years. Some people think that children remain unscathed by a death in the family and that a genuine sense of loss is just for adults. They are wrong.

My grandmother sobbed as we walked him to the graveyard. Mother was undoubtedly upset, but I don't know if I actually remember seeing her cry, or it's just the expected background for the funeral of a young husband and father. Perhaps my classmates were there, that would have been the done thing. After the burial, people came back to our house for tea and sandwiches. Neighbours were in the kitchen making gallons of tea and coffee. There were china cups and saucers with a flowery pattern; everyone was wearing black, carrying their cups with them from room to room.

Things were never the same again, and I don't just mean for me. Mother spent a lot of hours working in the petrol station and wasn't around much, while her Aunt May was around more than ever, helping out with meals and the housework. Grandma continued to bring me out walking, but I don't think she ever got over losing her youngest son. She was no longer the happy-go-lucky person who ran towards clumps of herbs and plants. Now she was sad most of the time. For ages after Dad died Auld Paul wore a black armband. Their son in New Zealand begged Grandma to come over for a visit while her daughter in Australia actually sent her tickets to go there, but she refused, saying she didn't want to leave me and Rikki.

I spent most of my time with Finn, my father's Alsatian. We would sit out on the porch for hours and hours, staring up the road, waiting – I understand now – for my father to appear. He was the one I cried with, the one I'd talk to about Dad. Every Friday, Grandma would bring fish for our dinner. Finn used to get so excited when he saw her coming that he would almost knock her over with his welcome. It was the high point of our week.

Every now and then I'd bring him to the convent orchard, to pick up their fallen apples. Whenever the nuns appeared Finn would bark and run at them, causing them to pull up their skirts and sprint as fast as they could back indoors. I couldn't help laughing; it really was peculiar to see nuns running.

I must have returned to school after Dad's funeral, but I don't remember. I was in fifth class by that stage. I also don't remember Christmas of that year; maybe we ignored it. Mother would have managed the business though we did have staff who worked for us at the filling station. However, Dad had been the sole mechanic, so I imagine that part of the business must have come to a sudden stop.

Sitting here now, all I can see in my mind's eye are the flames pushing through the roof of the caravan. Little did I know how much went up in flames that day.

CHAPTER THREE

Mother had been having an affair before Dad died. He was a farmer from Carlow who worked all over Ireland as a crane driver. He had stayed in Ardee a couple of times, in a Bed & Breakfast, and inevitably had his car filled at our petrol station. That's how they met. Years later I discovered that Dad had suspected it, following her one weekend to see where she was going. Frustratingly, I never heard what happened next. Naturally Rikki and I knew nothing, only that in the months following Dad's death we hardly saw her.

It was May and Grandma who did most of the housework and looking after us. Nobody mentioned Mother's frequent trips away though I'm sure that Grandma was as ignorant as we were, seeing how she had lost her son; that's why we were told nothing in case we spoke to her or Auld Paul. May, on the other hand, was most likely privy to every little detail.

Therefore you can imagine our surprise when Mother arrived home one day, about a year after Dad died, with a new husband in tow. As usual May was minding us. We were ordered to keep ourselves clean.

For me that meant staying indoors as I was wearing white ankle socks which were much too easy to smudge. I think Mother might have been away for a whole week because I can remember being immensely excited and impatient to see her again. I kept checking the window for *them*; May told us that she was bringing a friend home with her.

Finally we heard the back door open and Mother came into the sitting room followed by a man who had glaring blue eyes, a tanned, weathered face and grey hair. She was smiling and looked happier than I had seen her in a long time. 'This is Sean', she said, 'We've just got married, so he's going to live with us now.' Just like that. She didn't show us any wedding ring or give us any more information about it. Rikki and I said hello and he said it back to us.

I launched myself against the back of the sofa, to show Sean how I could do handstands. Since the back of the sofa was required to support my entire body I clearly wasn't very good at them at all. He said he had a trick for Rikki. He stuck a small magnet to the radiator in the front room and told him to wait a few minutes. Next he told Rikki to remove it. Rikki took it off and the magnet burnt his hand, making him cry.

He looked older than my thirty-year-old mother,

but that was on account of his rugged face, from spending so much time working outdoors. In fact he was two or three years younger than her. We looked at their wedding photographs. Mother was wearing a green suit and there didn't seem to be many guests. Today I still find it emotional that she hadn't wanted her children there. It was a big day and it feels like we simply didn't exist. As a mother I could never contemplate excluding my own children from my wedding day; it does not make any sense at all.

Aunt May stayed for dinner. It was a delicious meal.

From the beginning, Sean seemed to pay me special attention. He liked my handstands on that first night. He complimented my dresses, and the colour of my hair, which was auburn. A man of few words, he did, from time to time, make the effort to ask me how school was. Today I realise how hard this must have been for my eight-year-old brother. Sean completely ignored him. No matter what Rikki said or did, he never got a word of recognition or otherwise from Mother's new husband. At least he and I had one another. We were each other's best friend – for another while, at any rate.

I trusted Sean. Why wouldn't I? He was an adult and I was a shy ten-year-old who knew nothing about the world. Yet, something wasn't right. That feeling got stronger and stronger. As I look back now, I'm trying to decipher the different stages.

He touched me a lot. At first I didn't think about it, but after a while it began to bother me. When we sat down to watch television I would have to sit beside him on the couch and Rikki would sit on the other side of me. As the weeks passed, Rikki was dropped. It was just me; he would caress my knee and then, over time, his hand moved higher and higher. He would ask me to sit on his lap and would touch my hand in a way I found different and strange.

Things got worse when my mother got sick. They had been married almost a year at this point. Mother was tired all the time and needed to rest every day. When I asked her what was wrong, she said it was something to do with her blood. She even needed injections. It was all very puzzling until one day there was a cot in her bedroom. I asked her what it was doing there and was told it was for the baby.

I began to feel afraid, though I couldn't have explained why. The atmosphere in the house grew dark. That's the best way I can describe it. Visitors to the house dwindled away while the door to my father's garage now remained closed. I hardly saw my dad's parents anymore. Grandma stopped coming around and we were never brought over to her house apart from once or twice.

Mother was angry a lot, maybe because she was quite sick during the pregnancy. She had rhesus-negative blood which was different to the baby's. As far as I can remember, Aunt May also died around this time. I don't think we went to the funeral, I don't recall it at any rate. Really, it just seemed that lots of changes were happening. I felt like I had no control over anything.

Sean started to touch my chest despite the fact it was still completely flat. Now when he took my hand, he didn't just touch it, he used it to touch his own lap. I had no idea why.

I was excited about the new baby and set to work in school, making a blanket for it. It was blue and white. Sister Bridget helped me. Most of the nuns were sour or bad-tempered, but Sister Bridget was different. She actually chatted to me as we worked on the blanket. She asked me how I was getting on at home. Maybe she had noticed a decline in my appearance or manner. Perhaps she had heard about the new man of the house, or something about my mother's drinking. At this point I would still have been ignorant of the fact that Mother was frequently drunk and, besides, I would never have thought to confide any worries about my stepfather in a teacher, primarily because I would not have known how to articulate my growing uneasiness.

There had been a strange unsettling episode when he walked in on me while I was in the bathroom. The door could not be locked and after being tightly hugged and rubbed up and down by him I began to make my visits to the toilet as brief as possible.

Mother drank sherry. I noticed the smell first before anything else. It was sickly sweet and frequently on her breath. I remember when she would have been unusually friendly and happy. She would talk to me, plying me with questions about school and my day. It was nice and I didn't dare question it. When she wasn't drinking the television had to be off at a certain time. However, when she fell asleep in the early evening, Rikki and I could gorge ourselves on programmes like *The Brady Bunch*, *The Osmonds* and *The Monkees*. Between the complications of the pregnancy and the escalation in her drinking she was tired most of the time. She no longer played golf or went away for weekends.

When she went in to have the baby, her husband

took me into their bed. I was so afraid and didn't want to be there. I was also confused. What was going on? I was skinny and wearing my 'Peaceful Night' night-dress. He hugged me for ages and ages. That's all I remember. It didn't make sense to me. Why did he want to hug me in bed? He told me not to tell my mother and made sure that Rikki didn't hear or see anything untoward.

I began to hate how I looked. I hated my auburn hair that he continued to praise. When I looked in the mirror, all I saw was ugliness. When I look back now, I can see that he was implementing a system of preparation. For a while he had been coming into my room, when I was in bed, to say goodnight to me, which involved a lot of caressing and intense hugging. Despite my innocence I sensed there was something vaguely troubling about this.

I remember trips to the zoo, ice-cream cones and sweets. Sometimes he brought us to Mondello racing park which was probably his idea of heaven, such was his passion for cars.

He was precious about his pipe and had a whole ritual in the emptying and cleaning of it. Nobody else was allowed to touch it, nobody, but me. I was the chosen one who was trusted with cleaning the pipe for him. It was his way, I suppose, of showing that he found me trustworthy, in the belief that this would discreetly enforce my trust in him. And I did trust him, why wouldn't I? I knew nothing about evil yet.

When Mother came out of the hospital, she was suffering from post-natal depression – not that I knew that then. Her drinking got worse and worse. I think one of her doctors encouraged her to drink glasses of Guinness, to get her strength back up. He mustn't have realised she was on the road to alcoholism.

James, the new baby, had asthma and had to go into the Lourdes hospital where he was put on a nebu-liser. Little did we realise that this would be a regular occurrence each time his asthma flared up. Mother would get extremely upset, crying for hours on end and then wailing, 'Oh God, what will I do if he dies?' This terrified me and I would panic over him dying too. I began to spend most of my time caring for him because I was afraid he was going to die. My father had died so I knew now that this was a common enough occurrence. It was a definite possibility.

Like any woman, her handbag went everywhere with her. However, my mother's bag made a certain clanking noise and I could never work out what it was. Today, I know it was bottles of vodka.

Apart from the baby being sick it was a relatively happy time when Mother brought him home for the first time. Sean seemed to be pleased and would pick up the baby and hold him. He did work long days, however. He could be gone from early in the morning and even gone for days at a time. My mother's drinking would definitely be at fever pitch while he was away. Quite quickly, I became the baby's chief carer. It was me who fed him and changed his nappies and, as a result, he probably became the love of my life. I really enjoyed looking after him. In a way, this tiny being was my chief ally as Sean never touched me when I was busy taking care of James.

We didn't bother with family dinners in the same way anymore. Rikki and I only got to eat once my mother and Sean had theirs. The only time we ate together was Christmas Day. We didn't do anything as a family, not even watch television together.

Once we all went to visit Sean's mother and his family's farm in Carlow. His father had died when he was eight or nine years of age and he, as the eldest son, had taken over the farm. My God, but his mother was awful. Maybe she disapproved of him marrying a woman with two children. She made a fuss over James, her proper grandchild, but Rikki and I were not welcome and we were too young to understand that it was because we weren't blood relatives. I brought James out for a walk. On our return she cooed over the baby, asking him how he enjoyed his walk, while not giving me so much as a glance. At Christmas time she sent presents for baby James alone. Rikki and I just didn't exist as far as she was concerned.

I couldn't have known it, but I was being groomed. He used my mother as the tool to bond him and me together. For instance, if my mother was criticising me or complaining about something I had done, he would tell me to ignore her. If my mother called me stupid he made sure to tell me, when we were alone, that I wasn't to listen to her. Furthermore, he gave me alone pocket money, letting it be known that he would look after me, and that I wasn't to waste time asking Mother for anything.

He started this game with me, as if we were the best of friends, where he'd remain outside the house and flash his lighter in the window. This meant I was to go and meet him outside whereupon he'd ask me, 'Well is everything all right in there? Is she drunk or is she sober?' We'd have a chuckle together and I was glad to have him there to share the burden of my mother's behaviour. I truly felt he cared about me and my welfare.

Of course, I could not have known that there was a price to pay.

I was singing in the Christmas play. Most of the sixth class were involved since it would be the final one before we left primary school for secondary school. However, I had found out that I would be repeating sixth class so I was about to lose any friends that I had. Grandma had always told me I had a lovely voice and now I was going to get the chance to sing onstage. I really wanted Mother to be there. She had never heard me sing properly before. That night I saw everyone else's family sitting in the school hall, but there was no sign of mine. Somehow I managed to ignore my disappointment and sing my song.

Sean collected me afterwards. I asked him why they hadn't come. He said that James, who was now six months old, was sick so they couldn't leave him. What could I say to that. Then he told me that he needed to check on the cattle before we went home. He drove us to May's house. She was dead by now, but had left her house to my mother. Sean kept his cattle in the field around it. I hated the house even more now; it felt creepy and smelled bad. When we got to the house, he went inside, but I was too scared and stayed just outside the front door. He came back out to me and tried to kiss me, but I said 'Yuck!' Next he told me that he wanted to show me something in the kitchen and coaxed me through the front door. He led me into the kitchen where there was a big, solid table. He lifted me up onto it so that my legs were dangling over the side of it. Then he told me he wanted to see my knickers. 'Why?' I asked in surprise. 'I just want to see them', he said. I thought he was checking to see if they were clean. He reached under my school uniform and took them off me and then pushed me back on the table. I tried to push him back in turn, 'What are you doing? Stop! Stop!', but he didn't. Instead, he told me to be quiet and that he would show me what he was going to do. I still had no idea. Up to now penises, as far as I was concerned, were for going to the toilet. Up to now, I had only ever seen James's, when I changed his nappy, and it was tiny and funny looking. There was a light bulb above my head. It was bare, with no lampshade. I stared and stared at it while he wrenched my legs apart, pulled me towards him so that his body was at the same level as mine, pressed his hand hard down on my chest and began to push himself into me. The pain was excruciating. I pleaded with him to stop, but he ignored me and kept pushing. The pain got

worse and worse. I began to cry, 'You're hurting me!'
Tears were rolling down my face as he replied, 'Just
another little bit. Just another little bit.' He said that
over and over again. I tried to get out from under him,
but it was impossible to shift his hand off me. The
pain got so bad I think I actually blacked out because
the next thing I remember is the blood on my leg. I
didn't know how it got there and thought to myself,
maybe he's killed me. After that I vomited on the floor.
He handed me back my underwear and told me never
to tell anyone. On the drive home, he stopped at the
shop to buy me sweets. I was absolutely terrified of
him.

Fortunately I had no way of knowing that this
would be my lot for the next ten years or so: my stepfather raping me more than once a week, every single
week. From this point on I stopped thinking of him as
Sean. From now on he was McDarby, my stepfather,
my rapist.

At school, the next day, I was still in agony.
Fear stopped me from telling anyone. I knew what
McDarby did was wrong, but I was already starting to
blame myself, thinking, 'I should never have got out
of the car.'

CHAPTER FOUR

There was something about our house, or something in the house that came into being after McDarby moved in. What I mean is that I continually felt a shadow or a presence outside my bedroom door, but it didn't scare me. I just accepted that it was there and that it wouldn't hurt me. When I walked down the hall I would feel something brush by me, like a gentle breeze in the middle of our house. Also there were certain rooms that were always freezing cold no matter what, in particular my mother's bedroom. And then there were McDarby's cries in the middle of the night, 'Stop! Stop! Stop!' The first time it happened I thought I imagined his shouting. Apparently he had been pulled out of the bed and dropped to the floor. When my mother was drunk she would tell us that it could only be Dad. Whoever or whatever it was, McDarby was pulled out of bed on a regular basis. Mother had the house blessed many times by the local priest, but it didn't make any difference.

When James was about a year old I started to find empty bottles around the house. When I sniffed them the smell was so overpowering I would feel sick. Nevertheless I had yet to make the connection between the bottles and my mother's drinking habit. To this day I cannot listen to the likes of Johnny Cash, Willie Nelson or Neil Diamond. When she was drunk, she was either incredibly maudlin or incredibly angry and the music would be blasted throughout the house. It greeted me when I came home from school. She only played music when she was drinking. As Johnny or Willie sang out, she'd sing along, her voice slurred, and click her fingers out of time to the music.

If she was too drunk there was no dinner for us. A sure sign that the situation was hopeless was if I got in from school and the twin-tub was plopped in the middle of the floor. When it wasn't in use its rightful place was under the counter. Therefore, if it was out and she wasn't around, it meant that she had started drinking early and had gone to put on a wash, but found herself too drunk to finish the task and so returned to bed. The funny thing is that I grew to hate the washing machine before I learnt to hate her for her drinking. I suppose it was easier to hate the machine.

My life, as I had known it, was tipped on its head. I repeated sixth class and made few friends. It didn't help that all my new classmates were now a year younger than me. I had to sit beside a Traveller girl, who smelled. This wasn't her fault, but children can be mean. No one liked her because of the smell and few liked me any better. I got head lice from her and had to be doused with awful stuff that stank. On top of that, McDarby had me help out with the cows and calves and I ended up with ringworm. I developed a bald patch on my head and had to use a strong smelling cream. As you can imagine, none of this helped me to make new friends. The Traveller girl and I didn't speak much to one another, but I'm sure we understood how bad and lonely the other felt.

One evening, Rikki and I went to Grandma's. I don't remember where McDarby and my mother were, but my grandparents were minding us in their house. When it got late Grandma suggested we get into our pyjamas. When it got even later she decided to put us to bed which wasn't part of the plan, but certainly we had no problem with this. I don't know what time it was, but it must have been late since we were both asleep. I woke up to an almighty row. My mother was shouting at us to get up while Grandma pleaded to have us stay where we were. It was horrible. My grandmother was actually crying while we were frogmarched out to the car in our pyjamas. God only knows what else was said before the shouting woke us up. My mother was loud and aggressive when she was drunk. Making a scene wasn't McDarby's style.

We rarely saw my grandparents after that though poor Auld Paul did his best for Rikki and me. He hated McDarby; hated the fact he was living in his son's house and running his son's business. The great pity was that my grandfather began drinking more and so wasn't taken seriously when he raged all over the town about McDarby being a horrible bastard. I honestly don't know how much my grandparents knew. All I know is that I never told them anything. Perhaps my grandfather had noticed a change in me and just had a suspicion about what might be happening; whatever it was, it propelled him into marching up and down, in front of our house, holding up a placard that read, 'MY GRANDCHILDREN ARE BEING ABUSED'. This got him arrested and bound to the peace. I'm assuming it was my mother who involved the guards as this would not have been McDarby's style. From then on, we were not allowed to see or talk to him and he was no longer allowed near the petrol station.

We were ordered to ignore him should we see him in the town. Soon after this he became a lollipop man. I'd see him in his long white coat and red 'STOP' sign as I went to and fro from school. We weren't allowed to talk, but I would sneak him a smile and a tiny wave. Sometimes he'd try to chat to me, but I was too frightened to stop. What I needed were eyes in the back of my head. When Mother caught me talking to him a couple of times she had slapped and screamed at me. For my own sake I was forced to avoid speaking to him.

Looking back now, as a grown woman, I see how hurt he was and how he tried to fight for us. He must have felt so oppressed and misunderstood. I imagine he drank out of despair for what he couldn't do for us. God bless him, but he weakened his fight with every fresh drunken episode. People in the town dismissed him as a drunk who was unable to accept his son's death. This was the harsh side of small-town mentality. I think every small town has its fall guy and for many, many years Auld Paul was that guy in Ardee. He was the one in the wrong while my mother and her new husband had the respect of the town's business people. Unlike my grandfather, they looked smart while my mother drove a brand new Jaguar, with the big house and lucrative petrol station on the Drogheda Road.

At least I got to spend some time with him when he was dying. I was about thirteen or fourteen years old at the time. The change in his appearance was shocking. He had always been a big, broad man from his years of carrying bags of coal. When he was much younger he was known as a tough man around town. Now his shoes were on the floor, at the end of the bed and he wouldn't get a chance to wear them again. In one corner was a commode as he could no longer manage the short walk to the bathroom. He was so small now, half the man he had been. I walked up to the side of his bed and looked at him, unsure as to what to do or say. Grandma told me to tickle his feet, so I did and was delighted when the house filled with his laughter. Then he reached for my hand and held it tightly. He tried to say something to me, but he wasn't able to. We stared at one another and I felt that he knew exactly what I was going through. That was the last time I saw him alive.

My days spilled into one another, with nothing much to distinguish one day from the next, apart from the fact that things were only getting worse and worse. Aside from everything else that was going on, McDarby kept a tight hold on the family finances. There was little money available for Rikki and me. We wore the same clothes and shoes over and over again.

For a while Rikki had to wear his wellington boots

coming into summer, because his shoes had fallen apart. In fact McDarby seemed to take pleasure in tormenting Rikki in the most devious of ways, like removing light bulbs from his bedroom forcing him to be left in the dark; if Rikki plugged in a lamp, McDarby would remove the fuse from the sockets; if Rikki got his hands on a bulb, McDarby would wait till Rikki went to his room to read and remove the fuse from the fuse box.

On the coldest winter days there would be no heating as the oil tank was rarely refilled – due to her drinking, mother was oblivious to the cold. Home was no longer a place of comfort and holidays were some-thing we could only imagine. However McDarby had no shortage of money, and as new gadgets or tools came out he would immediately buy them for himself, indulging himself in trips to Mondello race track and spending money as he wished on classic cars, while mother spent what she had on alcohol.

Mother had just about given up cooking too. It seemed to me that our world revolved around his wishes. I hated him. I hated her.

When she drank she either got extremely angry or extremely sorrowful, which meant hours and hours of crying bouts. There was no in-between stage and certainly no party atmosphere, in spite of the loud music. Her rage was terrifying. When Rikki was about twelve she sent him to the shop for a bottle of sherry. On the walk home he somehow dropped the bottle and obviously had no choice but to admit it to her. She went crazy, there's no other word for it. He didn't want to, but she made him go back to the shop and fetch another bottle.

I honestly couldn't choose which was worse: his controlling every aspect of our lives or her alcohol-fuelled frenzies. Over time McDarby would help me to calm her and get her to bed, but it wasn't because he wanted to help his wife. Once my mother was tucked up in bed and dead to the world, he could do what he wanted with me. He concocted his way of summoning me. He'd head outside and flick his lighter on and off in front of the living room window. In the early days that had meant me sneaking outside to be asked what state Mother was in. Now it meant something different. Now the lighter flashing in the window meant that I was to make my way next door to my father's garage, which was now full of McDarby's junk, to be raped. Afterwards he would give me pocket money, buying my body and my silence.

Naturally I developed a pressing need to keep

my mother sober. He couldn't do anything to me while she was around, or at least it wasn't so easy to get at me. I risked her wrath as I embarked on my campaign to empty the bottles of drink I found strewn throughout the house. Once, out of curiosity, I had a taste from one and dipped my tongue down the neck of the bottle. Whatever it was, it numbed my tongue immediately. I couldn't understand how or why she would want to drink so much of this awful stuff. I got so desperate that I actually on a few occasionas asked different off-licences not to sell any more drink to her.

Christmases quickly became part of the nightmare. She made sure she had extra drink in so there was no way to limit her intake. The dinner was a disaster. Although we, like everyone else, bought extra food she managed to ruin most of it. Every year something burned to a crisp because she had got so drunk. One year the entire turkey ended up in the bin. I remember the second Christmas after he came to live with us; it was Rikki and me alone in the front room on Christmas morning. They didn't bother to get up until midday. I had asked for a doll and typewriter, but there was just a typewriter sitting on the couch, a blue one with tall keys.

It got so bad that we had to start hiding the knives

from her as she was getting increasingly violent when drunk, and was liable to physically attack any of us for no reason at all. I never stopped telling her what she had done. It was always the same. The day after the shambles of the day before, I would describe how violent and mean she had been. She would get remorseful, say sorry and promise to change, but within a few hours she was drunk again, screaming abuse at the top of her voice.

She went through a phase of ringing the guards when she got drunk. She said she needed help and they did turn up quite a few times. I supposed they were obliged to check up on her. I would answer the door, bring them in and show her lying on the ground out for the count. The strange thing is that I don't remember them asking me if we were okay. Our mother was out for the count and it was just me and my two younger brothers, one who was just a toddler. She really scared us when she was out of control.

I hated her.

I hated him.

I hated me.

I couldn't stop him from raping me. This was what upset me the most. He was much too strong to fight off. This was how I began to turn on myself and lay the blame firmly at my own two feet; that I physically could not stop him.

I became desperate enough to try to tell my mother, though I hadn't quite worked out how or what to say. Then, one night, I watched some programme on television, I can't remember what it was, and the girl in it said she had been *raped*. There was blood all over her, her clothes were ripped and her face was covered in mud. Furthermore she looked really scared. It dawned on me that this was what was happening to me. I had a word for it now, 'rape'. Keeping in mind I was only about fourteen, I felt that imitating the character in the programme would enable me to express myself. So I mucked up my face. In fact I went out to the bushes, in the back garden, and thrashed my face against them so that there would be scratches and blood. I needed to get bloody and torn, just like the woman in the programme. I rubbed muck on my face; next I ripped my t-shirt and messed up my hair. At the last moment I remembered that the woman had been out of breath and frantic.

I was now dressed for the part. Mother mustn't have been too drunk or I would never have gone through with it.

I raced into the sitting room. The fire was lit and she

was sitting on the couch. Neither McDarby nor Rikki was around. I acted frantic, telling her, in between gulps of breaths, that I had just been raped. Surely McDarby wouldn't touch me again. That's about as far as I got in my thoughts. Of course, she did have drink in her though she wasn't incoherent just yet. Her response was damning. She gave me a filthy look, snarling at me, 'Who raped you? Look at the state of you! Go and clean yourself up. What sort of tramp are you!' I told her that I didn't know who had raped me because it had been too dark to see his face. She lost her temper and was shouting at the top of her voice, 'Get out of my sight! Liar!'

Suddenly terrified at what I had done, I ran back to my room. What had I been thinking? I should never have said anything. He had told me not to tell anyone, that no one would believe me anyway. And he was right. In the bathroom I washed my face and asked myself over and over, 'What have I done? Oh, what have I done?'

Nothing ever came of it. I was fortunate that McDarby did not come home and I'm sure she never bothered to tell him about it. Even if she had, no doubt he would have merely complimented my over-active imagination.

So I continued searching for and emptying bottles of vodka while she continued screaming abuse until she finally fell asleep. There was little or no housework being done, no cooking whatsoever. To be honest it was better that way. When she did attempt to make dinner she would forget about saucepans burning away on the ring while she sang her heart out to her records or else went to bed to sleep off the drink.

In bed she'd start singing her other song, 'Mary, Mary, help me. Mary! Mary!' This could be repeated for hours on end. I'd have helped her to bed, tucked her in and then, within fifteen minutes or so, she would start calling for me, over and over and over again. I'd have to help her to the bathroom and back to bed.

When I wasn't in school, James was now my full responsibility and, in a way, she was too. It wouldn't be possible to count up the amount of times that she fell or scalded herself when she was drunk. Often I'd get in from school and find her with a bandaged leg or arm from some accident earlier that day.

Looking back, I don't think I coped too well. I did my best. I made sure James was fed and I emptied the bottles of vodka. Rikki usually escaped to Grandma's to eat there in peace. I didn't learn to cook until James was three or four so before that, if Mother was in a drunken stupor and McDarby wasn't around, it was either beans on toast or else I'd put James in the buggy and sneak down to Grandma's. Thanks to my mother this was no longer the pleasant visit it used to be, as I wouldn't have been able to relax for a minute, being constantly terrified that she'd wake up or McDarby would come home early.

The house disintegrated into a mess. School and minding James were full time jobs. I didn't have the time to dust or vacuum.

My mother was addicted to alcohol and couldn't get through the day without it. Most of the time she swayed as she walked and needed to grab hold of doors and furniture to stay upright. Her speech was slurred, but even worse than that she continued to drive her Jag. I hated getting into the car with her and she did have a few accidents. I emptied more bottles than I care to remember, but, sometimes, it was just easier to let her drink it. When James was about five, she brought him with her to Dundalk Shopping Centre, but then forgot about him and drove home. We were all in a panic wondering where he was and she was just too drunk to remember. Eventually there was a knock at the door; it was the guards who had found the child wandering about and brought him home safely.

When I was about fourteen years old my mother went into John of God's Hospital to be treated for alcoholism. Her violent behaviour had reached a new level and she was now physically attacking McDarby as well as terrifying her children. She signed herself out after five days and did seem to ease off the drink for the next few days, but it wasn't long until she resumed her drinking pattern. The five days she had been gone were a particularly low point for me. I had to stay home from school to mind James. She was gone, Rikki was at school. He raped me from behind. I was in so much pain I wanted to die.

McDarby was also getting violent with me. He took to hitting me because I would threaten to tell on him. So, I still had some fight in me. The lighter would flash in the window and if my mother was still awake I would cause a row with her to keep her awake. Especially on a cold night, I would do anything to stay in the living room where at least the fire was lit. It was freezing outside and it was freezing inside. If my mother was in a drunken stupor I had no way of denying him. There was no escape.

Sometimes I'd close over the door between the

sitting room and the kitchen window so that I couldn't see the lighter being flicked on and off. I could never forget that he was there. Mother might be still up, but he'd let me know that he was waiting. The door would be pushed open and he'd fasten me with a cold, hard stare, not needing to utter a single word. I was stricken with fear. A cold dread trickled over me and eventually I'd go out to him, just as he knew I would.

I did try to run away a few times, but I was always found out. I'd hide over in Grandma's, but Rikki would be sent to bring me back. Once I even hid myself in the confessional box in the church. It proved to be as cold and uncomfortable as the house. It was always Rikki who was sent to find me and fetch me back making him feel horribly guilty, but he was too young to do otherwise.

By now McDarby had become much more physically aggressive with me. I was in my first year in secondary school and McDarby was doing his utmost to keep me from having any kind of a social life. Every night he came into my bedroom to 'tuck' me into bed and tell me that he loved me. He'd insist on kissing me and groping me. I suppose he was afraid I'd tell on him and didn't want me out of his sight. Therefore, everything was 'NO'. NO, I couldn't meet friends after school; NO, I had to come straight home after school; NO, I couldn't go to any discos. Usually I never even got to finish the sentence so he didn't even know what he was saying no to. Mother wasn't much help. It was like she had relinquished responsibility to him. Having said that, once when I wanted to go to a school disco, which would have been well supervised, she did ask him why he had refused to let me. 'She might get herself into trouble' was his reply.

I loved to watch *Top of the Pops* and I was a huge Bay City Rollers fan. I even had my own pair of platform shoes (shoes again!). If I disobeyed him in any way I would be forbidden to watch it. Sometimes I was rewarded for my compliance with some pocket money or else I would be allowed some freedom, whether to watch my programmes or cycle my bike over to my friend's house.

Finally I managed to get to a school disco. It was wonderful to be able to temporarily forget about my troubles and, of course, nobody around me could have guessed what I was dealing with. I just wanted to enjoy myself and, in any case, I would have been far too afraid to share the truth with anyone. After a pleasant night my friend and I decided to go to the chipper on the way home. It was 10.30pm when I reached our back door. As I was about to open it McDarby appeared out of the darkness. He had been waiting for me behind the garage door. His face was hard, his eyes were cold and I could see the tension in his jaws as he asked through gritted teeth, 'Who were you dancing with?' One question followed after another. 'Why are you so late?' 'Who were you whoring with?' I didn't even know what 'whoring' meant. Of course I was as scared as he meant me to be, but I was determined to hold my own. Forcing myself to sound confident I replied, 'I just went to the chipper!' His reply was instant. He punched me in the face and then proceeded to do what he always did. When he was finished I somehow gathered myself together and went inside. Mother was drunk in bed so I just went straight to mine and managed to fall asleep despite the pain I was in.

The next morning my eye was swollen and a mess of purple and black. It was a school day so my mother used her own make-up to cover up the bruising. She was actually angry at him, demanding to know why he had ripped up my clothes and dumped my make-up. All I had was a little bit of eyeshadow and one black eyeliner and now even that was gone. It was in the bin along with my favourite tops that he had gone to the trouble of cutting up with scissors. Why on earth would he do that? I had so few clothes because he wouldn't provide enough money to buy me new things. His behaviour made no sense to me.

He was emotionally abusive too. Gone were the days when he would compliment me in the face of my mother's criticism. Over the months and years he often told me how stupid and ugly I was. 'Sure, who would ever want you?' was something I heard frequently. The unfortunate thing was that his words were accidentally confirmed by the fact Mother had already told me that Rikki was smarter than me. Naturally I completely lost faith in myself and believed that no matter how hard I worked I could never ever do any better.

From time to time he complimented me on my auburn hair. Well, this was something I could take charge of. I wanted so badly to escape his gaze. So one day I shaved it all off, accidentally cutting my scalp over and over again. I had to wear a cap to cover the scars. It was a small victory as my hair was never spoken about again.

When I was fifteen years old, McDarby explained what was going on when I discovered I was bleeding from a peculiar place. Mother's contribution was to inform me about the pack of sanitary towels in the hot press. He explained it was my period and that it would happen every month.

CHAPTER FIVE

Neither Mother nor my stepfather approved of my friend Dessie for the simple reason that he lived in a council estate or, as they put it, he was from 'up there'. Despite this I saw Dessie at least a couple of times a week as we walked to school together and back home again in the evenings. It was an easy friendship. Sometimes we walked along in silence, not feeling the need to talk if we didn't feel like it. Otherwise we mostly chatted about whatever had happened in school that day.

A lot of people were aware that Dessie knew how to stand up for himself. I used to sneak him packets of cigarettes from our shop and bars of chocolate on request.

One morning as we walked to school he said to me, 'God, you're getting stout!' I said nothing to this.

I was sixteen years old and my periods hadn't settled into a pattern yet. It was May and I didn't feel right. My stomach was round and hard as a stone and I felt ill, particularly in the mornings. Mother told me to visit the family doctor, Dr Birkette, who lived just across the road from us. He felt my hard stomach and advised me to eat bran. However, when I didn't improve, he made an appointment for me to meet another doctor, Dr Neary, who had private rooms in Drogheda. Mother drove us over. She stayed outside while this doctor examined me and then informed me that I was twenty-eight weeks pregnant. Stunned, I asked him how he knew this. 'Listen to this', he said. All I heard was a strange thumping sound. When I stared blankly at the doctor he told me it was my baby's heartbeat. He asked who was with me. 'My mother', I replied. 'Will I tell her or do you want to?' There was no way I could let him talk to her. She had been drunk for the fifteen mile drive from Ardee and always carried a bottle of Smirnoff in her handbag which she would have been drinking from while I was with the doctor so, all in all, it would be best if I checked how she was and then chose my moment.

'Well, did he know what's wrong with you?' she asked. I said nothing, preferring to get her outside before I said anything, not that I knew how I was going to tell her.

McDarby had already diagnosed my condition. A few days earlier I had come home from school, found him behind the garage and was desperate enough to ask him if he knew what was wrong with me. He smirked and asked me in turn, 'What do you think is wrong with you?' When I pointed at my swollen stomach – I hardly ate in those days – he told me I was pregnant, adding, 'I told you that I'd have you pregnant by the time you were sixteen.' I wasn't sure if I believed him and honestly had no memory of him making that sort of comment to me. My growing stomach scared me. I knew I wasn't eating enough to explain the roundness.

Outside, Mother and I walked towards the car park. I walked on the very edge of the path and stepped off the curb with every second step, looking as if I had a severe limp. My mind was limping along too. Do I say, I'm pregnant, or do I say, I'm having a baby! 'For heaven's sake will you walk properly and tell me what the doctor said!' As my foot went down on the step I blurted out, 'I'm pregnant! He said I'm twenty-eight weeks gone.' I kept walking, trying to look like it wasn't a big deal. Inside I was terrified. How could a baby be growing inside me, I'm too thin. Is it going to start eating away at me?

'Who's the father?' she snapped.

I hadn't considered her asking me this. Crap, what was I going to tell her? I couldn't tell her it was her husband. She wouldn't have believed me while I did believe him when he promised that he'd kill me if I ever told her. Since I was home just about every evening it was natural for her to conclude that I didn't have a boyfriend. Because I couldn't think up an answer I stayed quiet. She shouted all the way home, but finally let me be, thanks to the Smirnoff taking its effect.

It was the year of my Leaving Certificate. I wore baggy jumpers to school and fainted a lot. In fact this is mostly what I remember about the exams: fainting in the middle of one of them and the teacher having to get me a glass of water. Not one teacher or fellow student ever guessed at my true condition.

In the end, at McDarby's suggestion, I told my mother that the father was just some boy that I had only met once or twice.

Over and over again he warned me he would kill me if I told anyone. I was completely isolated. He made sure of that. I hardly went out at all. Nobody saw my bump because I hid myself away out of shame and fear. I spent hours of every day standing at my bedroom window, one foot against the other knee, like a flamingo bird, watching people walk up and down the main road. I saw everything. My bedroom was at the front of the house and looked onto the main road. If I wasn't doing this I was drawing boxes inside boxes, for hours upon hours.

McDarby continued to rape me while my mother ranted drunkenly about how she was so ashamed of me. It was not a happy pregnancy by any stretch of the imagination. James's cot was moved into my room. Most nights I lay awake wondering what on earth was going to happen to me. When I had a show of blood I didn't understand what was going on and started to believe that a monster or some sort of alien was inside me. I was so scared. It never occurred to me to get my hands on books about having babies. A walk to the library would have been out of the question. I was just too miserable and afraid. As it was, Rikki only learnt I was pregnant about four weeks before the baby arrived. At the time neither he nor I discussed how this had happened so I assumed he was blissfully unaware of my situation with our stepfather. Today he tells me that he did suspect something was going on, and he wanted to tell the guards, but he felt as trapped as I did.

I had a few check-ups and visits to the doctor's private rooms as McDarby wanted as few people as possible to know I was pregnant. On 26 October I woke up with back pain. When I told Mother she informed me that this was 'a sign' and told me to get my bag packed for the hospital. She drove me to the hospital and only came in long enough to sign the consent form. I was brought to the ward and she went home. At home McDarby informed Rikki, 'She'll be in some pain now!' And I was. The pain of the birth was unimaginable. I was skinny and the baby was big, over eight pounds. They gave me gas and air and the pain-killers of the day; I felt I was being torn in two. In fact that is pretty what much happened; I needed a lot of stitches afterwards. Going to the bathroom was utter agony and even just walking a few short steps made me feel faint. They kept me for twelve days because I caught an infection. Mother and Rikki were my only visitors. She was usually drunk. When she saw how ill I was, she loudly declared, 'If anything happens to you I'm not looking after that bastard!' I was too sick to respond.

I named him Oisín Ruardhí. I got the name 'Oisín' from a guy that passed by the house on his way to and from town. Because I had spent my pregnancy standing at my bedroom window, watching the world go by, he became a familiar face to me, unbeknownst to him. One day I asked Rikki if he knew him. Rikki nodded and said his name was Oisín. It was my mother who added the name 'Ruardhí', but in time I would simply call him 'Rory'. There was a nun working in the hospital and when she saw how sick I was she advised me to have the baby christened. Mother and Rikki were the godparents.

When they handed the baby to me, I just felt numb. I was a terrified seventeen-year-old who had just completed the Leaving Certificate not four months earlier. It felt absolutely strange to have a baby. I know I was a bit distant with him. Because of the stitches it hurt to lift him and also I had little energy, due to the infection I had. When the hospital finally told me that they were releasing me it was Sunday morning. I rang Ardee and my mother came to pick us up. I remember it was a Sunday because as soon as she arrived she began rushing me out to the car, telling me that she didn't want anybody in Ardee seeing us when they came out of mass. Such was her paranoia that, just before we reached the town she parked the car for a while, to be sure to miss the last of the mass-goers. She was not exaggerating when she said she was ashamed of me. However, she must have told Mrs O'Brien, who lived nearby, as she sent over a present for Rory. It was the only present we received.

Now I was well and truly trapped. I had to ask for anything I needed for the baby. As far as I can remember

I didn't receive any children's allowance and, therefore, was completely dependent on McDarby for every single nappy and tin of formula. Of course this was a way of keeping me under his control. How many times had he threatened to kill me if I told anyone? His brutality was growing. To be honest I am struggling to describe the strength of the hold he had over me and just how scared I was of him. From the age of ten I had been shaped to bend to his will, initially with kind words and gentle touches; now with rape, beatings and threats to kill me. He literally could do whatever he wanted; I had no way of stopping him.

When the health nurse called out to see Rory and me she was brought into the sitting room. The rest of the house was an absolute mess, but this one room was kept neat and normal for visitors which probably explained why she didn't ask me too many questions, just telling me to bring Rory to the clinic for his injections. In fact she might have thought I was lucky to live in such a nice house.

One friend visited me once after Rory was born. It was a rare occasion for me to have friends in the house. A couple of girlfriends used to visit, but McDarby would never leave us alone so they stopped coming around. I cannot tell you how lonely my life was. He had succeeded in completely isolating me. As we looked down on Rory, who was asleep in James's pram, she kept asking and asking who the father was. She knew I didn't have a boyfriend and rarely left the house. I had no idea what to say to her. I bent to fix Rory's blanket around him and said quietly that McDarby was the father. I couldn't even look at her face; I just heard her whisper, 'Oh God!' I asked her not to tell anyone for my own sake and safety. She promised not to tell another soul and I don't think she ever did, although I can't remember ever seeing her again.

When I brought Rory for his injections I snatched the opportunity of being outside to sneak a visit to Grandma, but she couldn't look at me. I couldn't understand why. In fact I had visited her once or twice when I was pregnant, but it was far from pleasant. What had I done wrong? Our relationship had declined by the time I turned up with Rory in the pram. It is something that troubled me in later years and I've had to think about it again in writing this book. Just last week I was talking to Rikki about her and he confessed that he did tell Grandma that Rory was McDarby's baby. I couldn't believe what I was hearing. He explained that he himself knew it was McDarby's baby and had considered going to the police, but then decided to confide in an another adult, Grandma. She told him that she could kill McDarby, but, of course, there was nothing she could do. I suppose I worried that she didn't want to know me anymore because I was pregnant out of wedlock and she was such a fervent Catholic. It was only in later years that I fully appreciated the awful stigma attached to unmarried mothers, because of the Church. Since the conversation with Rikki – over thirty years later – I now understand that she couldn't look at me because she couldn't help me and must have suffered over this. Why didn't I just tell her?

In any case my grandmother's reaction to me did have an effect on top of everything. I suppose it was a culmination of being a new, inexperienced mother who was still being raped and beaten by her abuser, my mother constantly screaming abuse in my direction and generally acting like she only felt hatred for me, along with Grandma's unexplained coolness that resulted in me deciding to run away. Tension in the house was at an all-time high since my mother had recently discovered that McDarby had forced himself on someone she knew, which had resulted in a baby. Of course the way Mother saw it was that her poor husband had been seduced. The house was a battle zone and I was living – or existing – on a knife's edge, in a constant state of fear and terror.

So, one night, I put Rory in his cot and packed myself a small bag of clothes. Everyone else was in bed asleep. I dropped the bag out my bedroom window and, as quietly as I could, climbed out the window after it. Gently, I shut the window after me and waited a couple of minutes to check that I hadn't caused a disturbance. I literally had no idea where I was going to go. Any time I ran away, in the past, Rikki was left with no choice, but to find me and bring me home again. For his own sake he would be thorough in his searching, trying the houses of a few school friends along with Grandma's and anywhere else he thought I might be. When he found me, and he always did, his face would be a mixture of relief and sadness as he hated the fact that he had to return me to McDarby.

I had no money with me and no plan in my head. All I knew was that I should just start running, which is exactly what I did. I ran and ran until I reached the other side of town, which was about a mile and a half away. It was all about getting away as fast and as far as possible. I stopped to catch my breath, which is when the panic took hold of me. What if Rory wakes up? What if his crying wakes up McDarby who would immediately realise that I had run off? Fortunately there was nobody around to see me. The town was as quiet as the house had been. I can't remember what time of the night it was. So here I was on the cusp of freedom, but trapped by my fear of McDarby and what he would do when he found out I had left. It was too much for me to deal with on top of the guilt of not being there for Rory if he woke up. Rightly or wrongly, I turned around and headed back, telling myself that I just wanted to check on the baby and make sure he was okay.

All was quiet when I reached the house and climbed back in the window. To my relief Rory was still fast asleep. As I stood there looking down at him, my heart still racing in my chest, I heard a sound outside my door. As quick as I could I jumped into bed and pulled the covers over me. The door opened and my stepfather asked, 'What were you doing?' I lay still, hoping against hope that he'd believe I was asleep. However he barged in and ripped back the covers to find me fully dressed. I was caught. 'Where were you? Who were you with?' He kept his voice low so that it sounded more like a growl, while his rage began to build and fill the room around me. I was so scared that I couldn't utter a single word, only numbly shake my head. I was suddenly overwhelmed by a need to sleep and was probably in some shock at what I had done – or had tried to do.

He began to roughly grope me. I begged him to stop, telling him that he would wake the baby, but this just seemed to fuel his viciousness. 'Where were you?' He kept asking that as he pulled off my trousers and then pushed me back on the bed, pinning my own legs against my chest, making sure I had no way of moving. I thought I was going to vomit from terror and pain.

I had to be quiet for Rory's sake as he rapidly plunged himself in and out of me, going as deep as possible. When he finished he sneered, 'Don't leave this house again!' and returned to my mother's bed, leaving me in agony.

Over the next few days and nights my stomach was sore with bad cramps, getting worse and worse. Unable to sleep I tossed and turned, thinking I had picked up some sort of bug. When I used the toilet I passed what I can only describe as brown fluid. I did briefly wonder if it was blood, but, no, it was definitely brown in colour. The pains were shooting through me, getting steadily worse, but who could I go to? I hadn't felt so much pain since giving birth to Rory a few months ago. What was wrong with me? I couldn't call my mother because she would have been no use to me and if he woke up I'd be either beaten or raped. Finally I thought to myself that perhaps I was dying. It certainly explained the level of pain. McDarby must have damaged my insides and, after five years of physical abuse, I was going to die. In fact I hoped I was dying; I even prayed to my father that I would die that very night although I hadn't felt his presence around me in a while. Death was the only way out as far as I could see.

I needed to use the bathroom and made my way there as quietly as I could. Almost doubled over with pain, I felt something move inside of me; I felt it change shape with each wave of pain. To my horror I felt something round pull out of me. When I looked I saw something that looked like a head hanging out of me as blood dripped down my legs. I felt light-headed and thought I was going to pass out. I had to get back to my bed and slowly dragged myself back to the bedroom, for fear of waking McDarby or Mother. I was convinced that my entire insides were falling out of me. All I could think was that there must have been some other baby in there with Rory and the doctors and nurses had missed it.

I never, for one moment, thought that I was

pregnant again and having a miscarriage.

As my entire body succumbed to the pain I didn't know what to do. Should I push it back inside me? I don't know how many hours I lay there, covered head to toe in sweat. My head pounded and my heart was racing. Whatever it was, it was inching its way out of me, bringing God knows what with it. It felt like gallons of liquid were streaming out of me. I wanted to die. I wanted to die. I wanted to die.

I had to be quiet. If I woke Rory he would cry and if he cried, he might wake them up.

Pulling my legs up to my stomach I tried to keep *everything* in, but, of course, I couldn't. After a long, long time I felt a big lump slowly push out against the inside of my leg. Too scared to look at whatever it was I gingerly pushed it away with my foot, as far as I could, and then curled myself up at the top of my single bed. It felt huge. The sheets and mattress were soaking, but I couldn't have cared less. I was beyond exhaustion, someplace else. As I gazed up at the ceiling I could swear that I saw it crack open, allowing a thin streak of light to come through. The room got brighter and brighter and I felt myself float up, up and away. The pain was still dreadful, but I was gone somewhere else.

The next morning Rory woke up and began to cry

to be picked up, but I couldn't do it. I had no energy and did not believe that I could stand up, never mind lift Rory out of the cot. McDarby appeared at the door wanting to know why I was ignoring the baby. I told him that something came out of me and it was down there. He pulled back the covers and saw that I was covered in blood and large blood clots. My nice pink nightdress was destroyed. McDarby looked at what came out of me, went out and returned with a large paper bag, 'Put it in there and bring it out to the garage. Don't let her see it!' I had to drag myself upwards. I saw the blood and stained covers, pulling them back I noticed a perfectly formed, tiny, translucent hand. The fingers were almost completely transparent, like sheets of tracing paper, my stomach sank and I realised, *it must be dead*.

I could only move very, very slowly. It took me a while to take off my nightdress and then I slowly wrapped it around the little figure. Dots danced in front of me. When I managed to slide off my bed I fell to my knees and the room started to spin again. God only knows how, but I managed to drag myself off the floor and put it into the paper bag. I'm sure I put on some clothes before I left my room and began the slow walk down the hall.

Thanks to its large windows the kitchen was usually the brightest room in the house. That morning I found it dark and full of ominous shadows. In fact, as I shuffled along the hall I felt a shadow walk beside me, the one that I always felt was outside my bedroom door. I was still in a lot of pain. My mother pushed by me on her way to the bathroom, and boomed in my face, 'WHAT'S WRONG WITH YOU?' I couldn't answer her and she had gone anyway. Closing the kitchen door, I realised that I had to be out of the kitchen by the time she got back. The back door was just a few torturous steps away. I had the bag in my hand and knew that McDarby was in the garage and he would take care of it. He waved at me through the window to hurry, but I wasn't capable of responding. I was barely able to walk. It was in the nick of time that I got out and closed the back door behind me just as I heard the kitchen door open again.

When I reached the garage I used the last bit of my strength to hand him the bag and then I passed out.

When I came too I was in the doctor's surgery. He gave me an injection while my stepfather told him that he didn't want my mother to know that I had been haemorrhaging. The doctor told McDarby to bring me to hospital. They kept me in for the next few days.

The consequences were far-reaching. From that point on I gave up; switched off; lost my will; died inside – whatever you like to call it. I became a machine. All my emotions vanished. I felt no pain, no relief, no guilt, no anger, no sadness and no love. The only part of me that kept working was my heart and I only knew this because my blood kept flowing. My brain and mind, however, were a different matter. I didn't care what happened to me now, I really didn't.

Not surprisingly I stopped praying around this time. So far my Hail Marys and Our Fathers had not helped me one little bit so it seemed pointless to carry on saying them. I felt abandoned.

The only option available was to switch off. Nothing mattered anymore. McDarby could do what he wanted to me or not. I didn't care. Mother could be drunk or not. I was past caring.

Because of this I have no sense of what happened in the weeks and months following the miscarriage. Well, aside from the fact that I was pregnant again, a short time later. I can't tell you if it was after he raped me once more or fifty times more. I hardly knew who I was anymore. I barely ate, barely slept and was barely awake. I minded Rory in that I fed him and James, and changed nappies and put them to bed, but that was it.

I wasn't a playful mother. There was never time for me to sing songs or read bedtime stories. It felt like everything was happening too fast. I managed as best I could and I also had to take care of my mother. Her drinking got steadily worse, if that was possible.

When I felt like I was too tired to carry on there was no one to look after me, so somehow I kept going. This probably explains why I hardly remember the details of Grandma's funeral. I was the one who had found her, dead in her bathroom, about a year after Rory was born, but that is about all I remember of this period.

This time I could diagnose myself as my stomach had swelled in the usual way about twelve weeks after the miscarriage. My mother might have tried again for a father's name, but I had no energy or interest in dreaming up someone new. She gave up asking after a while. I spent most of this pregnancy in a state of terror that I'd have another miscarriage and hid my growing stomach as well as I could. McDarby was my only option. I told him about being pregnant again and asked him what to say to Mother. His eventual solution was to move me out of my mother's house and Ardee. From that point on he controlled every-thing. When I was about eight months pregnant

McDarby told me he was bringing me to a house in Castleknock, in Dublin.

'But what shall I tell *her*?' This was my main concern. Mother didn't know I was pregnant yet. His threat to kill me should she find out was enough to keep me quiet. So, in effect, McDarby provided me with a solution, helping me to escape from her. He told me to say that I was moving in with my boyfriend. When she asked why she hadn't met this boyfriend of mine I said it was because of her drinking. Naturally she was drunk when I informed her I was leaving and it was McDarby who told me to blame her drinking. He knew exactly how to handle her. And I did whatever he told me to do because I didn't know any better. So, I suppose, he knew exactly how to handle me too.

I remember getting into the car. He had given me little or no warning that today would be the day that I was leaving home. Five-year-old James, who got upset if he lost sight of me for a second, screamed and screamed as I shut the door. He treated me as if I was his mother and depended on me for everything. I heard him crying in my head for hours afterwards. It was a horrible wrench, but I could do nothing about it. I was also leaving Rory behind, because the baby was due in a few short weeks and I wouldn't have been able to look after him, so I had to leave him behind. It may sound bad, but I found it much more distressing to be separated from James, now four years old, than from Rory. My feelings for this baby, a product of a brutal attack, were so conflicted.

I had never heard of the place, but it was a handy spot for him. Castleknock was on the main road from Belfast to Dublin. Drivers travelling to or from the North would frequent the garage there. McDarby pretty much worked all over the country, as operator of the biggest mobile crane in Ireland. The crane even made it onto the news back then. Castleknock was also convenient for his return to Ardee, taking the road through Ashbourne, Slane and Collon. Of course the fine motorways we have today were only a figment of someone's imagination then.

The only antenatal appointments I had were the two during the month that the baby arrived.

CHAPTER SIX

Ashley was born on 24 September 1983 in the Coombe Hospital in Dublin. I was dropped off outside the hospital and received no visitors or flowers or cards of congratulations. The woman in the bed next to me was calling her daughter 'Aisling', so I thought of 'Ashley'. She was christened in the church in Castleknock. This time McDarby asked his sister and her husband to be the godparents. It was a small, sad ceremony. I have no idea today what he told his sister, though I'd find it impossible to believe that they didn't think the situation strange. I mean, what else could they have been thinking? She was a timid woman who hardly said a word and stole brief glances at the baby. Today I wonder why we bothered even having a christening. It's not like we were celebrating. There was no party or special lunch after the church.

I hated Castleknock and hated the house. In my eyes it was too big. There was a little furniture in it, including a radio and a television. It was a new estate so everywhere had an unfinished look about it. Perhaps most of my neighbours worked because there were plenty of days when it felt like I was the only person left in the world. Rory was back in Ardee. McDarby would only bring him down to me every so often, but Rory naturally preferred the house in Ardee, the only home he knew. I was much too distracted to experience any loss in his absence. Ashley was born about a month after I moved in. Fortunately she was a good baby and didn't give me any trouble, but with the passing of each day I became more and more aware of how trapped I was. In fact I worried about Ashley because she was so good, too good. It had to be because I hardly showed her any affection, but I felt empty inside and outside. What I mostly felt was afraid. I had no money, no phone and not one friend in the whole of Dublin. The same dark shadow I had sensed at home was with me in Castleknock, but, to be honest, that just felt normal to me now. I hated my body. I hated my breasts. Perhaps I blamed them for what had happened to me. Sure enough four months after I gave birth to Ashley I was pregnant again.

I attempted to do something about it myself, with a silver wire hanger. It didn't work and I won't make you read the details. Today I realise that I probably would have tried the same thing on Ashley's pregnancy except for the fact I was too traumatised after the miscarriage. Iseult was born in Holles Street Hospital in October 1984. As with Ashley, I only attended maybe two antenatal appointments. McDarby chose the hospitals, wanting a different one each time so that no questions would be asked. Her name came from a book my mother used to talk about, called *The White Owl*. I remembered there was a princess in the story called Iseult.

He usually visited me every second night, to force himself on me, but, I was past caring by this stage. My mother didn't question his whereabouts as he always travelled with the job and up until his own mother's death, he'd frequently visit her too. Sometimes he'd even spend a couple of days with us. Now, away from my mother, he was free to abuse me whenever he wished.

After Iseult's birth the health nurse suggested that I go to a place called Cherish, a centre for girls who found themselves pregnant and had little or no support from family or anyone else. Maybe she mentioned it because I was from the country and was unmarried. Maybe she sensed my desperation. I certainly didn't share my story with her; that would have been unthinkable. I only went a couple times, driven there by McDarby. How else would I have got there? I'd imagine that he only brought me in case the nurse checked up on me and started asking more questions.

At some point I met another young girl, through Cherish, who was in need of help. I offered her and her children the spare bedroom. She had been thrown out by her family after having children with a black man. They only stayed for a few months, which was fortunate because it was chaotic in the house. The constant shouting and screaming became unbearable. However, while she was there, he couldn't do much to me so there was that. I don't know if I told her he was my stepfather. Maybe she thought he was my husband. We didn't talk about it either way. It was a mad time, but it strikes me today that perhaps I was starting to come out of my self-induced coma, but there was such a long road ahead of me.

My life turned into a series of changing nappies, washing babies, feeding babies, washing bottles, making bottles and so on and on and on. What stands out is that I developed an overwhelming fear that the children and I would be hurt by an intruder. After Rory came to live with us I believed that someone might break into the house at night. Therefore I took to locking us all into one of the bedrooms, with a hammer by my pillow. I didn't sleep much. When the health nurse visited us I'd be surprised if she didn't sense that something wasn't quite right with me.

I became a freak about keeping things neat and tidy. It was my way – my only way – of making sure that everything *looked* normal. Most of my days were spent cleaning. In the morning I'd start in one room and work my way through the entire space before moving on to the next room. Windows, ledges, shelves, the mantelpieces, floors, walls, toilets and the doors were cleaned every single day. I simply didn't allow myself to rest. Once I used something I would have to wash it immediately and put it back in its proper place. So, if I allowed myself a cup of tea, I would have to wash, dry and put away the cup as soon as it was empty. The sugar spoon would be washed and back in its drawer before I took the first drink. Of course this was my way of exerting some tiny control over my world. The radio had to be on all the time to distract me from thinking too much while also providing company. In fact the radio was perfect company; it was the only thing in my life that didn't make any demands on me.

At the weekends I washed my bottles of shampoo. The curtains were washed every week, as were the sheets on the beds, whether they had been used or not. The oven and the fridge were scrubbed out on a weekly basis. If I came across a speck of dust in any of the rooms I would have to start over again. When the kids were in bed I washed their toys, every night. I didn't have a vacuum cleaner; I just had one of those old carpet-sweepers and that got trotted out every evening for a thorough going-over of the entire house.

When the weather was good I'd sweep my way around the outside of the house, up into the back garden and then out to the front. And when I wasn't doing any of this, or attending to the children, I'd constantly be mopping the floors.

Today I wonder at the amount of energy all of this would have required. How did I manage to keep going? I would never have described myself as a nervous person, but it strikes me that maybe one of the reasons I kept doing housework was because I was too afraid to leave the house. I'm really not sure why I was so scared. My only reason to leave the house would have been to shop for food. Roselawn Shopping Centre had a Quinnsworth, but it was quite a distance away. Because there was still building going on and a lot of the paths were broken, I never wanted to risk it. As far as I was concerned, the estate was too much to cope with on top of everything else. I felt like a tiny, defenceless mouse living in that big house in a massive estate.

I missed home. Does that sound strange? What I missed was the sense of familiarity. At least in Ardee I knew the area. I knew the house – my father's house – his shop and the garage. There was the church, the lane to Grandma's house and the local shops. To be honest, I wasn't ever sure where exactly Castleknock was in relation to Ardee and the rest of the country. It felt like I was miles away from all I had ever known. Apart from all of that there was the fact that, as bad as she was, my mother was a sort of buffer between me and her husband. As horrible as her verbal abuse was, naturally I preferred it to his violence and sexual abuse. He couldn't touch me when she was awake. Also James and Rikki were there too and he couldn't abuse me as much when they were around.

Rikki and I never spoke about my children, how they came about. We were both too miserable and terrified of our stepfather to reach out to one another for help. I had no idea what my brother knew or didn't know and was much too busy to be curious about it.

In Castleknock there were few obstacles to getting what he wanted. He had little enough to do with the kids. He never helped wash them or feed them and he certainly never changed any nappies. The house was like my own prison and he was my jailer. He actually told me I wasn't to leave the house if he wasn't there. However, one time, I was really stuck for food for Ashley and Iseult. I dressed them and put them in the buggy which took ages, as any mother knows. I can't remember, but I might have been pregnant again. Whatever the reason was, I remember that the walk to Roselawn Shopping Centre took much, much longer than I thought it would. I pushed the buggy as fast as I could, so fast that I ended up with a stitch in my side, but I couldn't allow myself to rest. At the supermarket I got the food and was back out the door within minutes. By now I was frantic that he had called in and found the place empty. Of course I never had any warning when he was going to visit. He turned up whenever he liked and I had to be there, and that was that. I kept up a lightening pace despite the pain and the bags of shopping. Finally I got home. He wasn't there, but that didn't stop me from fretting that he had called in and would be coming back to punish me. All of this horrible stress for baby food! I can tell you, I didn't do that again in a hurry.

I hated hearing his car in the driveway, but also I was usually relieved. This is tricky for me to explain, but I did depend on him. When he visited it meant I could get shopping in and buy whatever I needed for the kids. I was living in his house and he was providing for me and his children. So, as much as I dreaded his key in the front door, I could also relax about the empty presses, knowing that they were about to be filled – relatively speaking – once more. When he drove us to the shops I was warned not to waste any time. As I got out of the car he'd mutter, 'You have forty minutes!'

Generally that was the extent of the conversation. That or 'This place better be clean when I come back.' There was no chit-chat, no half-decent conversation. I'd do my best to be upstairs with the kids whenever he turned up. He'd come in and, maybe, watch the news, make himself a coffee and corned beef sandwiches in silence. All he was interested in was dominating my mind and brutalising my body. When he did speak to me it was to tell me that nobody else would ever want me because I was so ugly. And I believed him. Because he was the sole authority in my life, having groomed me since I was ten years of age, raped me two years after that and then steadily disconnected me from my grandparents, my friends and even Rikki. Quite literally I had no one else in my life, only babies to take care of.

I regularly begged to be taken home to Ardee and when I got there I'd do my best to stay there for as long as I could. Once or twice I toyed with the idea of running away, once I even went as far as to climb out the window and walk a few yards down the road, but I couldn't leave the children. What if one of them woke up and I wasn't there? Who would feed them and take care of them? There was no one else to look after them.

Rikki wasn't home much so I hardly saw him when I was in Ardee. He did ask me once where I was living, but I was afraid he'd give my address to my mother, who wasn't to know where I lived, so I just said I was living in Dublin. Recently Rikki and I were talking and I discovered that he approached McDarby and asked him for my address. McDarby gave him one and Rikki travelled down to Dublin, in search of me. When he knocked on the door he couldn't understand why the owner of the house didn't know me. Back in Ardee, when he confronted McDarby he was told I must have lied about my address because I didn't want him to visit me. McDarby poisoned our relationship and we grew apart, not knowing any better. Why did we believe that horrible man who did nothing but lie to us all?

I never stopped being absolutely terrified of my stepfather. Furthermore I was so ashamed. I believed the abuse and the consequences – the babies – were my fault; that I could have tried harder to fight him off. All I did was repeat the word 'No!' over and over again which achieved absolutely nothing. In reality, there was little I could do, beyond keeping the house spotless, the children fed and try to prevent myself from developing as a woman. I didn't want big breasts or womanly curves and the only way I could achieve this was to not eat. At the root of anorexia is usually a desperate person trying to exert some power over themselves and their life, but, of course, I didn't know this at the time. My focus was on making sure the kids never went hungry. I was not my alcoholic mother who forgot or was incapable of cooking a meal. However that duty, or consideration, did not extend to looking after myself. So I went without food in an effort to keep myself as small as possible, in the barely conscious hope that he would leave me alone.

It didn't work.

In the fog or bubble I existed in, sometimes I'd actually forget that he was the source of all my problems in the first place, just because he was the source of food and necessities and had taken me away from my mother. In writing this I am torn between calling him Sean, my stepfather, or McDarby, the rapist.

CHAPTER SEVEN

At twenty-one years of age I had been through three painful births and a traumatic miscarriage. I was still living in Castleknock bringing up three young children by myself: Rory, Ashley and Iseult. And I was pregnant again.

My memories of this pregnancy are vague: I remember only that I was huge. By this stage I was barely managing. My daily life revolved around the bedroom containing my hammer and the walk to the kitchen to fetch food for the kids. When the weather was warm I let them come out to the back garden while I hung clothes on the line, before quickly returning to the house.

I still absolutely expected the house to be broken into. Throughout the night I tiptoed to the top of the stairs to see if anyone had broken in yet. The upstairs lights were left on all night, every night. It wasn't about me getting hurt. I was petrified that if someone broke in they could hurt the kids and I knew I wasn't strong enough to protect them. I even wondered if

McDarby would interfere with the girls. In fact I asked him about it. He replied that he would never 'touch blood'. I was only his stepdaughter, which made me fair game as far as he was concerned.

One time, when he stayed over and I was forced to lie beside him the entire night, I waited until he fell asleep. When I was sure he was out cold I decided to take my revenge and kill him. I reached for the hammer and without any hesitation hit him square on the forehead. He woke up immediately and I went to hit him again. He grabbed the hammer out of my hand and dropped it on the bed, staring at me the whole time. And then, just like that, he went back to sleep. Maybe he hadn't woken up properly and I had been very lucky. I decided against ever trying that again. The next day he made no mention of it.

Somewhere deep inside me I knew I had to do something concrete. I reached a decision: I was not going to mind this baby. Iseult had been a 'crier' and I couldn't face going through that a second time. Once again I felt I had reached rock bottom.

It was either November or December when McDarby brought me to see someone at the Coombe Hospital in Dublin. My memory is vague. There was a big desk and a woman, a social worker, sitting behind it. Perhaps I made up a fantastic story as to why I wanted this baby minded. Who knows, maybe I even told her the truth – I was certainly desperate enough – but I can't recall the details of the conversation.

She mentioned a home in Blackrock where the baby would be minded. It was a home for unwanted babies, or babies who would, in time, be adopted. I didn't know this; all I wanted to know was that 'it' – the outcome of this pregnancy – would be taken away and cared for until I felt strong enough to mind it. It was a short-term solution to my immediate problem.

I was huge on this pregnancy. I wasn't eating much and was shocked at how big I got. The bigger I got the more I hated myself and my body. It was hard to move around, but with three kids under the age of four I just had to get on with things. Looking back today, I honestly don't know how I managed, but I suppose it was down to the fact that I literally had no choice.

Christmas 1985, McDarby brought me home to Ardee. There were no decorations and no tree, but it was better than being alone. Apart from looking after the kids, I was kept busy hiding knives and emptying my mother's bottles. I would describe it as a typical family Christmas, but the fact was, the drink was taking its toll on Mother.

The kids were too young, but I still wanted to buy them some things. The only money I had was whatever he gave me, or sometimes Mother gave me a little. Of course shopping was never a simple pleasure for me. I needed a lift to Dundalk to buy the few presents, or whatever I needed for the kids. She would drive me over and I would be in fear for our lives. At the shopping centre I'd try to concentrate on my shopping, but invariably I also had to keep an eye on her. I didn't want her going to the off-licence to buy more drink. And then there were her frequent trips to the toilets to drink her vodka. I hated going shopping with her; it was a nightmare. I had to be fast so that she wouldn't have time to drink too much, so I never got to browse or window-shop.

I felt trapped, as it was painfully obvious to me I was completely dependent on my alcoholic mother and rapist stepfather. They were the source of my money and since I could not drive I was forced to rely on them for that too.

My mother's drinking curtailed her curiosity about my life. She did ask me where I was living and I just said Dublin. I really wanted to tell her more than this, but his threats hung over me. I kept hoping that she would give up drinking and become the sort of mother who would help me and support me, and protect me. I so badly needed a 'real' mother, but she just wasn't available in this way. She seemed to accept that I had had more babies, but was too drunk and befuddled to do anything except rant in her usual way. It might be hard to understand that we never sat down together at the kitchen table and had a cup of tea. We never chatted and she certainly never asked why I kept having all these babies. As a mother she was useless. I was so used to her abuse and rage that it didn't make any difference to me anymore. I felt old and worn out.

On the evening of 1 January I went into labour. I had to wake up him and my mother to ask for one of them to take me to the hospital. McDarby drove to me the Lourdes Hospital and dropped me off at the gates, not even waiting to see if I made it to the front door. As usual I was on my own. 'It' finally arrived during the night – a boy weighing 10 lb 2. No wonder I was so big. A nurse tried to get me to feed him, but I didn't want to. He lay in his cot beside me, but I didn't want to look at him.

I kept insisting that I needed to get to the Coombe in Dublin. That's all I would say. The Lourdes rang the Coombe to tell them I was on my way and I rang McDarby to come get me. It was either the day after the birth that he drove us to Dublin. I sat in the back seat, holding the baby in my arms. McDarby had named him Andrew. I studied him, but could not find anything inside me to connect with him. It was as if I was looking at him through a thick pane of glass. I just couldn't do it anymore. I had nothing more to give. I was there in body only, my spirit was elsewhere. I get so sad when I think about my lack of feelings for the innocent little boy.

As usual, McDarby dropped me outside the hospital. Because I came from a different hospital, the baby and I were put into a separate room on my arrival. The nurses kept trying to get me to feed him; I did eventually give him his bottles. A day or two later a nun arrived and made arrangements for me to bring him to the home. McDarby brought me; he questioned why I was doing this. I replied, 'I just can't do this anymore.'

Within a week or so I was back in Castleknock, only now I had to visit the baby in Blackrock once a fortnight. McDarby always took me, but he never came in. He took no part in my decision to have him minded. I can't say if he cared one way or the other. At the home I was brought into a room and the baby was placed in my arms. For the duration of my visit I would just sit in silence and stare at him. No maternal feelings developed over the course of these visits, except sadness. This was not Andrew's fault. In a way I think it was my attempt to stand up to my abuser and say 'no more, I'm done'. The christening took place in the home and comprised Rikki and me. I don't imagine we said much to one another. We were both too lost, too miserable and would have been incapable of describing or sharing how we felt. I didn't get to see where the baby slept and had no idea who actually looked after him all day. I hated the feeling that I was a bad person; I already hated myself so much.

Coming to Blackrock was another task I had to perform on top of looking after my other three babies and toddlers. As the weeks turned into months ,the staff told me that they hoped I could take him home soon. They also explained they were having him examined over the way his head constantly flopped. He had no hair on one side of his head while on the other side the hair was pure blonde.

The problem was I just couldn't cope, and they couldn't really keep him if I was going to hold onto him. I hadn't really thought beyond having him cared for when he was born. When they explained that adoption would mean I'd never see him again, I was torn. For as long as I could, I put off doing anything.

Then, when he was eight or nine months old, the home told me they couldn't keep him any longer. That was that. I had to go and bring him home. McDarby brought me. Still I felt no attachment, no connection to him. He needed physiotherapy, so I still had to go to Blackrock once a week. McDarby drove us there and back.

He was a big baby and very strong. When I held him he constantly wiggled and pushed against me. All I had was a travel cot and he had no difficulty getting out of it. He cried a lot, I remember that, and I do have the odd flash of his blonde hair and his constantly watching me. Unbelievably I do have a couple of photos of him after everything else I've lost over the years. It wasn't his fault that he came at such a difficult time for me or that he reminded me so much of McDarby.

I felt so ashamed of being an unmarried mother. All the hospitals I had been in, all the staff that had ever dealt with me had – I believed – thought me a bad person for getting pregnant. I mostly blamed myself for my situation. The guilt and the shame never left me. I imagined dirty looks and whispered conversations along the lines of 'Well, of course *she* got pregnant, what else would you expect?' Andrew was yet another innocent paying the price, along with his siblings and myself.

Weeks kept passing and turning to months, but it made little difference to me. However, it was around this time that I did make a couple of attempts to leave.

One day I packed my bags and decided I was going. I didn't know where I was headed; I just knew I was leaving. To be honest I wouldn't even have known how to get a bus. Because I couldn't leave the children, I had to wait for him to show up. When he put the key in the door I stood in the hallway, suitcase beside me on the floor. He saw it immediately and looked at me. I said 'I'm leaving!' His expression was smug; he didn't take me seriously. In order to get to the front door I had to pass him. He practically filled the hallway and issued his challenge, 'Go on then. There's the door!' His tone matched his menacing expression. I just wanted it all to finish and I felt it might if only I could pass him. The front door was open and the world outside beckoned. He was the sole obstacle to my freedom: a living, breathing and snarling metaphor. My feet were stuck to the ground. I was frozen in fear. It felt like my blood was cold in my veins and yet, somehow, I willed my legs to move towards him. Tears filled my eyes as he lunged out at me, his fist catching me full in the face. I crumpled to the floor in front of the children, who started to cry. I sobbed all the way through the beating.

I couldn't pass him. I had tried, but I simply couldn't: mentally, emotionally and physically I was trapped.

About a year after Andrew was born McDarby organised a 'family' holiday. I had asked to go home to Ardee, but he said no to that. Instead he borrowed a mobile home from a guy he worked with. It was in Enniscrone in Sligo. This was my first holiday ever, not that I got a chance to relax. The mobile was tiny and barely contained him, me and the four kids: one-year-old Andrew, two-year-old Iseult, three-year-old Ashley and almost five-year-old Rory.

He dictated exactly how we spent our days. I watched other families happily traipsing off to the beach, but we weren't allowed that freedom. We did get to the beach alright, when he felt like it, but he drove us there, despite the fact that the caravan was in the sand dunes, right next to the beach. It was a two-minute walk that we never got a chance to do. At the beach I could take the kids out onto the sand, while he stayed in the car and supervised us. There was never a minute when I didn't feel his eyes on me. He didn't talk to us and we didn't talk to him. The kids and I were literally not allowed out of his sight the whole time we were there. When we weren't driven to the beach, the kids played on the little square of grass in front of the caravan while I was allowed to sit on the steps to watch them. And when I wasn't doing that, I was cooking for everyone and washing clothes and cleaning kids and the inside of the caravan. The children weren't afraid of McDarby, but it was only Ashley who ever tried to make him engage with her, calling his attention to something shiny in the sand and receiving at best a terse nod of acknowledgement.

I remember standing on the water's edge and staring out across the ocean, wishing and wishing I could cross it. I knew it was the Atlantic Ocean and that America was on the other side of it. It was on this 'holiday' that a seed of an idea was planted in my brain.

CHAPTER EIGHT

I was recently asked if I loved my children back then. It is a difficult question to answer. I certainly cared about them; I fed them and looked after them to the best of my ability. However, I hated myself so much. I hated who I was and hated my life. I hated having to keep secrets: my entire life felt like one great big, dirty secret. I hated that I couldn't stop him from raping me. This was something that I've had to remind myself of then and since: I could not stop him. I could not stop him. I COULD NOT STOP HIM.

I hated the air I breathed. And I believed McDarby when he told me I was ugly. So, I don't know that I would have been capable of 'love' at this point.

Around the time of bringing Andrew home the house in Castleknock was put up for sale. McDarby had to find me another one. He moved me to Mulhuddart, into another rented house. This one was smaller than the Castleknock house. It had three small bedrooms upstairs while downstairs comprised the kitchen at the back and the living room to the front.

McDarby handled everything, so I honestly don't

remember much about the move or the general area, other than there were more houses around me. It felt different from Castleknock, and also I didn't have any shops near me. The kids were a little older and, therefore, a little more difficult regarding keeping them stuck inside all day. Not that I really remember, but I assume that I continued doing hours of housework as always. Plus I still slept with the hammer beside my bed.

My nextdoor neighbour was married to a garda. She was a friendly, chatty girl who might have been a little older than me, but we struck up a friendship over the back garden wall when I went out to hang clothes on the line. Her son was the same age as Andrew. Our friendship would have been all her doing, since I would have been paranoid about talking to her or anyone else. McDarby still threatened to kill me if I told anyone the truth and I still believed him. To ensure that I didn't get caught, I probably made a point of only hanging out clothes bright and early. It would have been too risky to get into conversation with her in the evenings. In other words, I felt no safer in Mulhuddart than I had in Castleknock.

However, there was another reason that I was nervous about talking to anyone: I imagined that people on the road were curious about my situation. McDarby looked years old than me and I was convinced that the neighbours were talking about me behind their front doors. I always made sure that the kids were dressed nicely and the girls had their hair in pigtails. It was my way of making things look normal, or trying to at any rate. I'm sure my new friend knew there was something wrong. All we ever did was chit-chat, but I think I might have come across as being perpetually afraid. Later she would say that she noticed my bruises and was truly concerned about me.

As soon as he saw how friendly and chatty my neighbour was he'd run her down to me, calling her a tramp and ordering me not to tell her anything. Then she asked me to come out with her and her friends. Little did she know that my agreeing to go represented a huge step for me. We ended up in the Garda Club, where else! I had a terrible pain in my tummy which I recognise today was probably fear. It was extremely weird to be out at night and in a friendly, social setting, which for anyone my age who hadn't gone through what I was going through, and had children as a result of abuse, would have been such a normal event, hardly worth mentioning. People came over to talk to my neighbour and I was a little overwhelmed. Because of

McDarby I believed I was too ugly for anyone to be the least bit interested in me so that certainly played havoc with my self-confidence. Honestly, I hardly knew what to do or say for myself. This pleasant night was so, so far removed from my ordinary life.

One thing I do remember is that any time I was introduced to someone, my first thought was whether they could help me escape from McDarby. Now, maybe this was because I was in the Garda Club and was presumably surrounded by gardaí. In any case it surprises me today; that as soon as I experienced something akin to a social life, all I could think about was getting help to run away.

I never told my friend that I wasn't allowed to go out, but I thought that because her husband was a garda, McDarby couldn't really say anything. I was determined to be brave. I had a couple of drinks and got a little tipsy, but I wouldn't allow myself to get drunk. I didn't want to talk about my life, and also, he was back at the house. Sure enough, when I got in, the kids were in bed and he was waiting for me. It was late, I don't remember the exact time, but I was later than I said I'd be. He never said a word, there was no row or screaming match; he just stood up and silently beat me. Of course he was clever enough to only thump me about the body where the marks wouldn't be seen, he rarely touched my face. However I was so used to the beatings by now that I didn't cry out. To be honest, I was numb to his cruelty.

That was the first time I went out with her.

The second time I went out I met more of her friends and, I think, her cousins who lived in Boston. One guy, gave me their address and told me to look them up if I made it over there. I can hardly remember anything about them today, other than that one of them was really confident. I think I wrote to them a couple of times after they went back to the USA.

I also came into money at this stage. The petrol station was being leased out and Mother told me I was due a little money. When Dad died he left everything to Rikki and me, while Mother was allowed to live in the house for the duration of her life. She contested the will and had the house turned over to her, leaving the petrol station to be divided between my brother and me. Then, when the garage was leased out, the money was entrusted to the solicitors. I got a thousand pounds. So, that was something.

Looking back, I think I was a little stronger in Mulhuddart. The house across the road had a play-school and the health nurse said it was a good idea to allow Rory and the two girls to attend it. They were such good and quiet children. I began to let them out the back garden to play and then out the front too, something I had never done in Castleknock. Andrew was a real handful in comparison. He was always opening and emptying presses, constantly on the prowl, like any eighteen-month-old learning to explore the world.

One thing that I am glad to confess is that I wasn't a harsh disciplinarian with the children. I certainly would not have been able to slap them or treat them in any way that reminded me of my mother or their father. I suppose I didn't want them to be scared of me; I was scared enough for all of us. For instance, I have one vague memory. The children were playing in the kitchen and I stepped out into the back garden to quickly hang clothes on the line. I swear I couldn't have been gone longer than four or five minutes! I returned to the kitchen and found that the girls had emptied a box of washing powder all over the floor. I mean it was *everywhere*. My reaction was one word, said calmly, 'Bold!' And that was it. I started cleaning it up and they moved onto something else.

In any case they were good kids. I made sure he never had to say anything to them either.

When the kids started playschool they knew he was their father, but they never called him that. It was just one of those words that were never spoken in our house, which was a good thing since they certainly couldn't call him 'Daddy' in Ardee. I hardly spoke either whenever he was around. His visits were very quiet indeed. Other people commented on how quiet the girls were and I'm sure they learnt it from me.

At the same time I was definitely struggling. My exhaustion was always with me and getting in the way of the housework. Cooking, washing, tidying and cleaning every day was getting harder and harder. The only break I got was the infrequent visit home to Ardee, which wasn't exactly enjoyable, but was at least familiar.

CHAPTER NINE

America struck me as being too far away for McDarby to get at me. My neighbour and I began to make plans for my escape. I can't remember what I told her, but I am pretty sure that I wouldn't have shared my entire story with her. I was too scared of McDarby to do that and also wasn't ready to tell anyone the truth yet. Whatever I did tell her prompted her to suggest that I contact social services, but I wasn't up to this, so she rang them for me and arranged for a social worker to come out to her house to meet with me. Meanwhile ,I needed a passport. This was complicated by the fact that I was born in England. I found my birth certificate in Ardee, but I had to prove that I was Irish. I needed both my father's birth and baptismal certificates to prove he was Irish. Nothing was ever easy. I had to do all this snooping behind McDarby's back, but I finally got everything necessary and applied for my first passport. Now it was just a matter of booking the tickets.

In the midst of this, the social worker came out to Mulhuddart. I needed help. We met in my friend's house in case McDarby suddenly showed up. It was still nerve-racking as it would have enraged him to find me elsewhere, no matter who I was talking to. I could not stop him, but perhaps someone else could? Could she have my kids taken care of? She sat down on the very edge of the chair, took out her notebook and her pen and I told her that my children were the result of years of being raped by my stepfather and I couldn't cope anymore. She was older than me and seemed to distract herself from my story by writing copious notes, her observations, in her jotter. She didn't share her opinions with me. As I spoke, I was obliged to address the top of her head and she rarely looked me in the eye. She didn't exactly inspire confidence and I had to force myself to keep talking.

Thanks to my lack of emotion she couldn't have guessed my terror as we sat there. I felt I was possibly creating a huge storm that I had no control over. This was the first time I had reached out to someone official. It was a huge ordeal to tell her about the children's conceptions and to be constantly on the alert for the sound of his car in the driveway. He had promised to kill me if I told anyone and, here I was, breaking his golden rule.

I didn't bother mentioning the miscarriage or

some of the more horrible aspects of the rapes, yet I sensed I had overwhelmed her. At some point she suggested a refuge house, but I knew he'd track me down if I stayed in Ireland. I wanted to be safe from him. I wanted not to be hurt anymore. She couldn't seem to understand that. All I really remember is her telling me not to do 'anything stupid' – whatever that meant. It still puzzles me today. Suicide wasn't an option; it didn't present itself as a way out of my situation. Going to America was an escape, but if she truly thought I might be considering killing myself why did she merely get back into her car and drive off, leaving me alone to continue trying to deal with McDarby and look after the kids? I also remember that she didn't look me in the eye when she said this. Neither did she suggest calling the gardaí and having them come to my aid. Her visit was pointless. And it bothered me that she had sat on the absolute edge of the chair as if about to flee herself at the first opportunity. In no way at all did she commit herself to me or the children. How different things might have been if she did.

There was no follow-up visit.

The solicitor in Ardee gave me some money from the garage and I used it to buy my first airplane ticket. All I knew was that I was going to Boston.

I didn't cry much about my life. It seemed a waste of time, but I made up for it as I counted down the hours to leaving Ireland. The evening before I left, I cooked sausages for the kids' dinner. I kept turning the sausages under the grill long after they had burnt. I just kept turning and turning them and I cried as I did it. Then I cried as I served them to the children. The day I left remains one of the worst days in my life and I certainly had my fair share of those. The kids were so quiet that morning and didn't give me an ounce of trouble. They usually were good, but everything felt different that day because I knew it was all coming to an end. As far as I was concerned, this was probably the last time that I'd ever see them. I fed them, washed them, dressed them and took my time to comb and scoop up the girls' hair into pigtails, leaving not one strand out of place. Finally I brought them across the road to the playschool. My friend was going to pick them up and hand them over to McDarby who was due to visit that night. She already had Andrew because he was too young to go to the playschool. If McDarby didn't show up she had his number at work. I had a fierce pain in my stomach. It was like someone was pushing a stick through my stomach and forcing it up my throat. I don't know how I managed to say the word 'Goodbye' and pretend that everything was normal. The three of them went inside and I got myself to the doorway and broke down, keeping my hand over my mouth so that no one would hear me. Several years would pass before I'd allow myself to cry like that again. It felt like my heart was cracking into shards, but, at the same time, I had completely convinced myself that the children would be better off without me. In desperation I prayed to Grandma for strength while simultaneously doubting that she'd want to help me, even if she could. I was no good as a human being; this is what I truly believed.

It wasn't easy. As I sat waiting for the plane to take off, I was terrified that he was going to miraculously appear and prevent me from going. When the plane finally left the ground I was terrified that he would come after me, despite that fact that I had no idea where I was going. All I had was one address, but I didn't know if anyone there was going to help me or not. I must have thought McDarby was bionic or had superhuman powers. The terror was absolute. When I wasn't thinking about him, I was thinking of the kids. God knows why, but I felt they'd not even notice I was gone, never mind miss me. I honestly didn't think I mattered to them. It shows you how far gone I was. I remember I had a couple of drinks on the flight in an effort to calm my nerves.

At Boston airport I felt myself starting to panic again. What was I doing here? I knew nobody. I asked where to get a taxi and, clutching the piece of paper with the all-important address in one hand and my small suitcase in the other, I took the escalator down to the ground floor, all the while gazing about me in fright. All I had ever known were white Irish people and now I was surrounded by all types of people of all nationalities and all complete strangers to me. The airport was huge; I had to fight to keep calm. Gathering myself together, I found where to change my money into dollars and then headed outside to join the long queue for taxis.

I had done it; I had made it to America.

The house looked rather rundown and it was an effort to leave the safety of the taxi and walk up to the door. Again I wondered what on earth I was doing here. I didn't know these people and they didn't know me. I rang the bell and someone let me in. There was a group of friends sitting around watching television; drinking cans of Budweiser, all around my own age, including the guy I had met in Ireland, so that was something. For a moment or two I was bewildered.

All that I had gone through to finally make it here –
the abuse, the fear, saying goodbye to my children, the
busy airports, being completely alone in a new country
– and it was for this, to find a bunch of people just
watching TV and drinking beer, hardly curious about
who I was or where I had come from. I didn't know
what to do with myself and just squeezed in among
them without saying a word. I couldn't have realised
that this was the norm. There was a constant flow from
Ireland of friends newly arrived, or friends of friends
or, like me, the barest of acquaintances. To find a place
to stay you only needed an Irish accent.

I was offered a drink and took one, listening to
them talk about where they were heading that night.
Apart from nodding and smiling I made no contribution to the conversation. Eventually they settled on a
pub called the Purple Shamrock. It was assumed that I
was going out with them. I asked the guy what to do
with my case and he told me to leave it there. At least
Now I knew where I was staying that first night and
could relax a bit.

I remember little about the bar except that there
were rows and rows of brightly coloured drinks. When
the barman asked what I wanted, I just pointed at the
orange one. The noise was tremendous and I was glad

for it; I didn't want to think about home. This was fortunate, as over the next few weeks I was constantly surrounded by noise. We went out most nights and if we stayed in we watched MTV, the music station, at full volume. It suited me. I have a vague recollection of one or two of the guys trying it on with me, but I didn't like it.

At one of the bars I got chatting to a group of Irish girls, who told me that the place was looking for staff. They encouraged me to approach the manager and I got the job right there and then, thanks to my experience of working at the petrol station and shop in Ardee. They also told me about an apartment full of Irish people who would probably take me in. They were right. Rent was fifty dollars a week. So I now had a place to stay and a job. At another bar a guy asked if I wanted to buy a line. Thinking he meant a sponsored walk or a raffle, I asked him what it was for. Smiling in disbelief, he asked me where I was from and hearing my answer, explained he was selling cocaine, a line of cocaine.

I discovered joints when I was living with the girls. *What a strange looking cigarette*, was my first thought. I didn't know which end to light up. However, when I did, I loved it. I fell around the place laughing, feeling happier than I had ever felt in my entire life. I couldn't get enough of it and it had to be pointed out to me that joints were for sharing, otherwise I hogged the whole thing for myself.

A friend of a friend, a biker, introduced me to cocaine. He brought me to a house party. I had no idea where I was, but there were lots of Harley Davidson bikes parked outside. We walked into the living room and I saw a big pile of white powder on the coffee table. When I asked what it was, my new friend told me it was a drug called cocaine. Intrigued, I asked what it did. 'It helps you to loosen up and talk', was the reply. I took it a few times over the next few hours, but my friend remarked that it seemed to have the opposite effect on me, because I didn't say anything at all. In fact the only effect it had on me was that it made my throat feel tight.

About three months after I arrived, I rang home to Ardee to see how the kids were. Rikki answered the phone and told me that the girls and Andrew had been taken into care in Dundalk because I had 'abandoned them'. He sounded upset and angry with me. By this stage our relationship had deteriorated, thanks to McDarby. My visits to Ardee had been infrequent and when I was there Rikki was usually elsewhere.

My brother had rung social services himself because nobody was looking after them. McDarby was doing nothing for them and my mother's drinking was the same as ever. Rikki was only nineteen years old and felt he had no choice. He did it for their sake. My mother held onto Rory because she didn't know he had also been fathered by my stepfather, her husband. Of course this meant that Rikki was taking care of Rory as best as he could, as well as looking after Mother when she was drunk. How could he possibly care for the others as well. I was overwhelmed with guilt and shame. Rikki told me I was to contact the children's social worker in Dundalk. Well, I couldn't – I was terrified. Instead I left the girls and their apartment and the job and began my wanderings for the next few months. I was literally on the run from my life.

I moved around, took up odd jobs, while consuming drugs and my favourite cocktail – B52s – whenever I could. One time I took the drug LSD. I had no idea what it was or what it did; it looked like a bit of dust on a piece of paper. Nothing happened for the first few minutes, but then, rather unexpectedly, I saw my own head fall off my neck and roll away. I watched it in fascination and, to be honest, it made perfect sense to me because I was carrying so much crap in my head:

of course it had to fall off at some point and roll away as far as it could get. Sure, how else was it going to find peace?

Not surprisingly I was too desperate to be interested in relationships. I had a lot of friends, male and female, but I just hadn't the headspace for anything else. One guy liked me enough to ask me out on a date. It turned out that he just liked Irish girls while I had little interest in him, but we went out anyway. A couple more dates followed and he tried to get physical, but I wasn't capable of it. I lay there, my arms across my chest while he asked what had happened to make me like this. I never told him, but was upset to discover that, even in his eyes, there was 'something' wrong with me. I couldn't bear to be touched; I didn't even like my hand to be held.

I was drinking far too much for someone my size. The big advantage of working in bars was that I could depend on getting a few free drinks every so often. I also hung out in a lot of Irish bars where friends or acquaintances worked. One bar served such strong Long Island Iced Tea cocktails that the rule was only one was allowed per customer. Thanks to my friend, who worked there, I had two or even three and this was probably after drinking lots elsewhere. A famous Irish singer, who I didn't know, began his session, singing some fiddle-di-li lonesome ballad and I just wanted to tell him to shut up. I hated that music. However, I was so out of it, my head was stuck to the table and I couldn't lift it up. I couldn't move at all. So I had to sit there and listen to it.

There was only one way I was heading and that was down. One night I went into the subway to get a train back to wherever I was staying. Three guys approached me. One of them held a knife to my face, saying, 'Give me your money, lady!' while the other two blocked any means of escape. They needn't have bothered. I looked the first guy in the eye and said, 'Take it!' I wasn't angry or aggressive; I just didn't care what happened next. And they could see that, which explains why he put down the knife and they walked away from me without another word.

Blackouts became a regular occurrence for me and I ended up in hospital being pumped out about three times. A female doctor, on my third visit, said, 'You are doing a very good job of trying to kill yourself. If I see you in here again I'm going to have to place you in a psychiatric ward.' She also sat in the room until I gave her the Ardee address because of all the money I owed them. In due course she sent the bill to Ardee, but it was never paid. Meanwhile I began to feel that Boston was getting smaller and smaller. I met so many different people, but didn't tell any of them who I really was. Nobody got close to me. When James, a friend of mine, asked what was wrong with me I told him that I had had a child and it died. If anyone else asked, I concocted a wealthy family that I needed to escape from because they wouldn't allow me my freedom.

I got a job as a childminder, to mind two children in their home. Not surprisingly, I quickly discovered that I couldn't cope with minding someone's kids. I was being constantly reminded of my own children and had to give up the job after a couple of weeks. However, I finally managed to ring the social worker in Dundalk, who told me that I had to write a letter giving them permission to put the girls into a foster home. And I also had to write a letter stating that I wanted Andrew adopted. I did what they told me to do because I figured I wasn't coming back home.

I wasn't like any other young Irish 'Paddy'. I didn't go to America to get a good job and find a nice apartment. I wasn't chasing the American dream or looking to be a success in some way. I had no ambition and no interest in finding the perfect career. As far as I was concerned, America was purely about escaping my life of misery in Ireland. Every drink I took was to block out the kids' faces. I told myself over and over again that they were fine and much better off without me – and when I was drunk I believed this, but I see now that I never managed to forget about them. I see today that I thought about them almost constantly and never stopped missing them.

While I was away my mother went up to the house in Mulhuddart and told all my neighbours that she was Sean's wife and my kids were the 'illegitimate bastards' of her husband. I assumed it was the social workers who filled her in.

One consequence of writing those letters for the social worker was that I never saw Andrew again. I find it extremely difficult to think about this. Why did I let that happen? Why did I not keep him when I kept his brother and sisters? What the hell was I thinking?, but that's just it, I wasn't thinking at all. There is not a day that I don't regret it, that I don't wonder where he is or how he is doing. Not one Christmas or birthday has passed without my thinking about him. I cannot describe what it is like not to know anything about his life today. All I heard was that he was adopted by a professional couple who were told the true story behind his birth. Even today when I hear the name 'Andrew' being called, I look to see if it's him.

I rang the social workers and wrote to the girls every so often to see how they were. Gradually it dawned on me that I'd have to go back. My life had turned into one long binge of drugs and drink with odd jobs in between. I befriended Native Americans in bars. They appeared rough angry men, but I was never afraid of them despite their rugged appearance and heavy drinking. I felt they weren't so different from me. We were outside 'normal' society, and wanted by nobody. I was in a bad state. One evening I was making my way to a train station – where exactly I couldn't say – and arguing in my head about going back to Ireland. The kids were the only reason to go home. They had their father in Ireland, but he proved unwilling to take any responsibility for their care. Yet they were my kids too and right now they had no mother because she was away, getting completely off her face, just like her mother before her.

Oh my God, I had become my mother. How did that happen?

The usual guilt and shame overwhelmed me and I walked with my head down, hardly able to bear my own self-hatred. I heard footsteps coming in my direction. Typically it was the shoes I noticed first. They were boots, moccasin-type with fringes on them. As they passed me I felt an incredible whoosh of air and looked up to see a huge Native American man, as broad as he was tall. He said, 'Go home. You'll be okay!' and was gone, just like that. I mean, he completely disappeared. I looked around, but he was nowhere to be seen. I was alone on the street, so I couldn't even ask anyone else if they had seen him or if I had imagined him, but I hadn't imagined him, I knew he had to have been real because I felt his message pierce me right through to my bones.

It occurred to me that I needed help with my addictions. The doctor who had treated me in hospital, suggested that I attend Narcotics Anonymous meetings (NA) as well as AA meetings. I went to my first meeting and it was full of homeless people. I felt sorry for them, but then it dawned on me that I was homeless too. I had to move constantly from place to place, sleeping on couches and dirty floors, and relying on friends or people I didn't know too well. Only God knew how long it would be before I ended up sleeping on the streets. Some of those people, at the NA meetings, became my friends. They even helped me get work, which I badly needed so that I could afford the plane ticket home. I had sold my return ticket ages ago; everyone did that to fool Immigration into thinking you had left on the date you originally promised to.

I worked in a few more bars and saved as much as I could. Eventually, thanks to my friends in NA, I had enough to buy my ticket, which I did. Next, I rang the childrens' social workers and gave them the date for my flight. I was all set. Only I wasn't, not really. My fear of McDarby and what he might do to me on seeing me again was increasing with every passing hour. I had been away for seven months and it was extremely difficult to volunteer to return to the old way of terror and pain. I went to the airport, checked in my suitcase and got my boarding pass, but that was all I could do. The plane took off without me and I never saw that suitcase again. Terror got the better of me that day.

A few weeks later, I was back at the airport and this time I got on the plane because I had no other option. All my money was gone and it struck me that I was homeless, without any real hopes that this was ever going to change. I had met a lot of people and some of them were lovely, but I never allowed myself to be honest with them and give them the real story of my life. Therefore I felt as lonely as I ever did. If you haven't been really and truly lonely then it is hard to convey how it can completely overwhelm a person. I just couldn't break out of the cage that McDarby had created for me. I mean, why couldn't I tell some of my drinking friends what I had been through? It was loneliness that sucked the hope out of me about things getting better anytime soon. For a brief time I considered suicide, only going as far as deciding on the method. If I was going to do it, I'd slit my throat with a Stanley knife because they were renowned for their sharpness.

I never had time to get 'into' music, but some of my friends were massive U2 fans. The album, *The Joshua Tree*, which came out that year, 1987, was one that was played for hours on end. After a while I'd put it on for myself and sit listening to it through the headphones. There was one song in particular that spoke to me, 'Running To Stand Still'. God knows how many times I listened to it, but I worked out that he – Bono – had written it about heroin. Now I preferred cocaine, but this song, I felt, described me: I knew how to scream without making a sound and all that running I had been doing was going to end with me getting on a plane and stepping out at Dublin airport, to go back to the horrible situation I had done my utmost to escape. In other words I was running to stand still.

A social worker promised to meet me at Dublin airport, bearing a placard with my name on it. I don't really remember what the plan was. They must have convinced me that I needed to be assessed and that's why they wanted to help me get back home to Ardee. On the flight I got chatting to an American, an older man who was visiting friends in Newgrange. He asked me where I came from, but had never heard of Ardee. Thank God! On and on he went, about how lovely Ireland was and all I could think was how much I hated it. All I could think was … *if it wasn't for the kids.*

At Dublin airport there was no social worker to greet me. I had no money, no nothing until the friendly American walked by and I told him that my friends hadn't turned up. He said that he was going to hire a car to drive to Drogheda, where he was staying, and kindly offered me a lift.

The nearer I got to Ardee the harder it became to breathe properly. I felt I was stepping back into a box. And so I was.

I got out of the car, thanked the friendly tourist and made my way to the house. Even before I reached the back door McDarby was there to meet me, 'Get in here, now!' I followed him into the garage where he gave me a good beating, all the while saying over and over again, 'I'll kill you if you tell anyone the truth' and then … and then he raped me. Of course he did. How could it have been any other way? He was the boss of me and that was that. I had been a fool to think I'd ever escape him for good.

When I finally made it into the house my mother was drunk. She took one look at me and screamed, 'Get out! You're a disgrace, a whore!' It was only then that I realised that she knew who the kids' father was and that she had made it her business to rant about it all over Mulhuddart. She had also discovered that he had had another child with the other person he had abused and, in her head, she lumped me and that person in together as having seduced her husband. (In time she'd get a barring order against him and completely ignore it herself.) Rory was there. He seemed okay, but I saw the fear in his eyes. Rikki was there too, my poor little brother. He told me he couldn't cope with all the kids and asked me why I had left in the first place.

And that was my first day back in good ole' Ireland.

I rang the social workers to tell them I was back and – boy – were they surprised. 'There must be a mistake', they said. Yes, there mostly certainly was. I had told them what plane I was on, what day I was flying back and pointed out that I had no money. So now, here I was, back in hell with no money, no transport, no decent home and no kids, aside from Rory.

It was my mother who drove me to see the children's social workers in Dundalk. As usual she was drunk and driving and, as usual, I was simply dropped off to take care of everything alone. It was my first time to meet them in person, but they were the pair, a man and woman, I had dealt with on the phone from America. The man said he was surprised that my kids appeared to be so well cared-for. I swallowed my anger at this. If there was one thing I knew for sure it was that I had always done my best to take care of my children. They explained that the kids were now wards of court because I had 'abandoned' them. There was that word again. If I wanted them back I would have to prove that I was a fit mother. In desperation I told them about the abuse and that the children's father was my stepfather, the man married to my mother. Their response is one that I'll never forget: they said that it was too 'unbelievable' a story to be true.

I hung my head in shame and felt they were judging me, convinced that they felt I had brought everything on myself, including almost a decade of brutal rapes. I didn't try to defend myself or explain things further, which would have required confidence I didn't have. It was so confusing. McDarby had admitted to having a relationship with me that began when I was thirteen. Why wasn't anyone doing something about this? Could it be that they thought the physical relationship was consensual, that I willingly had sex with him? Mostly I felt they didn't believe me and that was that. I was there to try and get my children back. Nevertheless, they advised that I approach the Rape Crisis Centre, to give me, I assume, the benefit of the doubt. They also told me that I had to find a place for the children and me to live. Perhaps it was too big for them to digest so they decided to focus their concern on the children.

The most important thing was that I – at the very least – must appear as if I was coping with life like any other human being.

CHAPTER TEN

I made the appointment with the Rape Crisis Centre (RCC), but didn't show up for it. McDarby's rage was constant and he told me that I was nothing more than a 'traitor' and a 'mouth'. Again and again he threatened to kill me if I told anyone else. Well, if I went to the RCC, as the children's social workers advised, I was required to do exactly that – repeat, once more, my story to strangers. Not surprisingly, I caved at the thought of it. Meanwhile Mother's rage was also constant, she could spend hours – and I mean that quite literally, *hours* – screaming that I was a 'tramp' and a 'slut'. So, no, I couldn't face that first appointment and had no one to advise me otherwise.

McDarby had been proved right. He had told me, over and over, that nobody would believe me – which was then unintentionally confirmed by the social workers when they described my story as being 'too unbelievable'. The world was closing in around me. It was probably worse since I had had a taste of freedom in America because now I knew what I was missing, even if I never felt completely safe and free across the water. My past was chained to my ankles and dragging me down. Furthermore I was genuinely bewildered when no one offered to stop my stepfather from abusing me any further. Why didn't anyone ring the police?

Dad's sister, my Aunt Josie appeared on the scene, having travelled from her home in England. Mother had rung her at some point. In fact Mother's new pastime was to get blind drunk and then ring anyone she could think of, to tell them about her tramp of a daughter seducing her poor husband. Plus, you see, it wasn't the first time. McDarby had impregnated another girl, so now I was lumped in with this other seducer while her husband remained more or less blameless even as she used make-up to conceal my bruises caused by his thumping my face. How did she not see what was going on?

It's strange, but in writing this book I didn't really know what to expect on an emotional level. This is stuff from the distant past that I had thought and hoped I would never have to revisit. Today I find I am absolutely enraged and, at the moment, it is directed at my alcoholic mother who failed me in every possible way. It is like a veil has been lifted. She knew I had tried to run away many times over the years. Did it not occur to her to be at least curious as to what or *whom* I was running away from? She saw the bruises, met the children and ignored them except for Rory, allowing them to be taken from her house into care. For some reason she refused to believe that Rory was also her husband's. Several times I tried to tell her the truth, but she was not about to take information from a liar and whore. Rory had even started calling her Mammy. Well, why wouldn't he? I had been gone for so long, but why on earth would her only daughter have disappeared to America in the first place; surely that struck her as something peculiar for me to do? Did she not see my misery? I was about six stone at this stage and spent hours in front of the television, in a zombie-like daze. Was this normal behaviour for someone in their twenties? But I was worthless in her eyes, not worth investigating and she was beyond feeling anything for anyone.

She knew bits and pieces. Apparently she had met up with social workers in Dublin, while I was in the States, but I'm not entirely sure how much she learnt from them. McDarby had had to admit he was the children's father in order for them to be taken into care. He had also admitted to being Rory's father, but Mother seemed stuck on not believing it. Meanwhile I was stuck. He still raped me whenever he liked and I had no idea how to stop him, no idea at all. It seemed like hate was all around me in Ardee. Rikki could not help me because he was so miserable over having had the kids taken into care. If he spoke to me at all he avoided my eyes. I did not think to tell him that I realised he had to do something since they were receiving no care in Ardee. There was no friend around to help me work out my options. I couldn't seem to grasp any control over my life. All I understood was that I wanted my children back.

For that first appointment with the RCC I was over in England with Josie. My Aunt's only remedy was to give me a break from everything. Aunt Josie was in her sixties and little able to offer real help. The situation was beyond her comprehension. She didn't like McDarby and then admitted that she had never liked my mother, especially after she discovered how Mother had been collecting Grandma's pension and using most of it to buy herself alcohol. This was news to me. Josie and Dad had been very close and she missed him as much as I did.

Fortunately she could afford to put herself up in a hotel when she came to Ireland. I hardly remember her visit though I know she came to Dundalk with me, to see the children. It was her way of being there for me. Then she took me back to Dorset and I honestly remember nothing of that. She was offering me a safe haven for a few days, but I would only have been too aware of how temporary that was. Seven months away in the States had been banished with a particularly horrible rape before I even got through the front door in Ardee.

I am not going to provide details, but I will say that when you read that McDarby 'raped' me, it was much, much more than him penetrating me. The attacks had little if anything to do with sex and they were usually extreme in their brutality, often leaving me doubled over in pain for hours afterwards.

About a month after my return from America, Mother drove me to my first visit with the children. I had expected to see Andrew too. He had been living with the same foster family as the girls, but when I got there I discovered he had already been taken by his new parents. I had asked to see my son, but was told it wasn't possible. Next I was driven to an office in either Kells or Navan where I signed my name on the dotted line. I told the social worker that if my child ever asked about me, or came looking for me, I was to be told immediately because I would want to see him again. It was all I could do.

Andrew was gone forever. So, it was just the girls. I couldn't wait to see them. Mother and Rory waited for me outside. As soon as three-year-old Iseult saw me she turned away from me while four-year-old Ashley hugged me so tight. I wanted to cry and cry until I was emptied out, but felt under pressure to look like I was coping. I was hiding everything now: the fact that my heart and body were broken, the fact that I had no idea what I was going to do and the fact that I was pregnant again. Yes, that welcome-home rape had produced another baby and I was scared that the social workers would think I was in a consenting relationship with McDarby, and therefore had lied about everything and didn't deserve to have my children returned to me.

Of course the girls asked when they were coming home. I explained that they had to stay with the foster family for another little while and then I would be bringing them home with me. It was so hard to say goodbye to them and walk away, promising that I'd see them again in four weeks' time.

As far as I can remember McDarby admitted to being their father, but said there had been no abuse involved. In other words he told the social workers that he had been in a relationship with me – his stepdaughter – that had begun when I was thirteen years old. My mother may have backed this up, but I'm not sure.

I do not remember being asked to provide any details about the abuse, or should I say 'alleged' abuse. That became the mantra of my sessions with the social workers, the 'alleged' abuse. Possibly the social worker didn't quite grasp my story or exactly what I had experienced. The focus was on getting the children back and I was going to have to prove myself as a mother and human being. Their father, my stepfather and rapist, was not required to prove himself in any way.

In my absence the children's social workers had invoked a 'fit persons' order and now I had my work cut out for me to have that reversed.

McDarby was not asked to provide me with a house or money. I had absolutely nothing, but I needed to get to the Rape Crisis Centre for the second appointment and show that I was a worthy mother. I had no money and two rotten alternatives to get to their Dublin address: either my mother's drunken driving or else accept McDarby's offer. He was presumably motivated by the fact that if I missed another appointment the social workers might get more and more curious about my situation. So, as crazy as it sounds, a rapist drove me to the Rape Crisis Centre.

As usual, he hardly spoke to me throughout the journey. How I hated the smell of that car; it stank of him and his pipe. He parked the car a little way down from the centre and pointed out the front door to me. As I got out of the car he issued me the usual warning, that he would kill me if I told anyone else about anything. My heart sank even lower, if that was possible.

Apart from terror and anxiety, I also felt utterly ashamed as I walked up to the entrance. I was appalled to see the sign over the front door that, in my mind, screamed out 'Rape Crisis Centre', in other words, it was telling everyone on that street that I had been raped, that I could not stop a man from raping me, that I was a victim. Plus I hated the word 'rape' and walking into the *Rape* Crisis Centre was like me making a big confession that I didn't feel ready to do. When I described my situation to the social workers I said I had been 'abused' by my stepfather and that he had 'been at me'. The word 'rape' was something I did not want to admit to. Perhaps I was still smarting from the one time that I had used it, when I hoped my mother would help me, only she had just screamed 'Liar' at me instead. I wonder what word McDarby would have used.

I kept my headphones on as I walked through the door and up the stairs, looking for a receptionist. Don't ask me today what music I was listening to, but it got me there. The lady at the desk took my name and let the counsellor know that I was waiting to be seen.

The door opened and a friendly, warm woman introduced herself as Mary C., my counsellor, but I could not relax with her. Physically she was tiny, and this troubled me because I found myself thinking, *how can she possibly help me? She's much too small to stop him from attacking me.* In any case she led me to a room upstairs and I did my best to hide both my fear and the latest pregnancy. Also, I felt I had to watch my every word since she was reporting back to the social workers in Dundalk. She did ask how I felt about the social workers, but I was too confused to give an honest opinion about anything.

At some point the two social workers came to see my counsellor and me a couple of times, although I honestly don't remember any details of these sessions. They were in regular contact with my counsellor, either by letter or phone. I assume they would have been checking my mental and emotional progress with Mary C, to see if I was ready to have my children returned to me. All I can say is that I would not have said much when I was with the three of them because I felt like a child at those meetings.

Everything was in a whirl. I was barely home from the USA and I was back in McDarby's hands, the attacks as frequent and as brutal as ever. My kids had been taken away and, on top of all of that, there was another new baby forming in my womb. Once again I had tried to abort the pregnancy, first with a clothes hanger and then with scalding hot baths. When that didn't work I wore baggy clothes to hide it from the social workers and this nice lady who had no idea of the hell I was in. I could not tell her who had driven me here to meet her nor could I tell her I was pregnant once more. Knowing that McDarby was waiting for me outside stunted any temptation to properly fill her in. I was absolutely convinced that he knew me inside and out and that I could never hide anything from him. One glance would tell him if I had confessed the truth. I did not know how to lie to him. So, I said very little indeed. It is difficult to hide so much from someone who is interviewing you for the specific purpose of finding out as much as they can about you. Oh, God, how I hated my life, hated him, hated my mother, hated Ireland and so on and so on.

Afterwards I walked out the door and moved away from that telltale sign as fast as I could. McDarby was in the same parking spot. Of course as soon as I got back into the car he asked or stated, 'I hope you kept your mouth shut!' I said yes and told him that my next appointment was the following week. That was the entire conversation for the journey back to Ardee. He was now the designated driver, bringing me to the centre once a week.

I didn't say much at the sessions, probably because I felt bewildered by the topic and my experience. I mean, which of all the rapes should I describe first? And what could I say about it, what point was there in discussing the times or the place? Mostly I just talked about my children and how difficult I found it to visit them under supervision at the monthly visits. I was so struck by the unfairness, that I was being supervised as if I had done something wrong. It was impossible to forget I was being watched closely as I tried to engage with the girls in front of their social workers, to try and chat to them about what they were up to without being self-conscious or making them nervous with me. I wanted to appear as natural as possible, to show I was a good mother or, at the very least, that I was doing the best I could under the circumstances.

My counsellor at the RCC, did her best to ask about the situation, but for a long time I refused to let down my guard with her. The social workers had passed on my information to her and I knew she would exchange her news with them. I did not like this. One time I asked her how often she was in contact with the office in Dundalk and she explained that she had to keep them updated with my progress. This prevented me from really trusting her because I was trying to hide so much from them in order to get the kids back. She was a good woman, but it was impossible for me to relax in her company because so much was at stake. I couldn't show her any side of me that might convince her I was unfit to be a mother. For instance there was no way for me to confide that my rapist had driven me to the centre and was outside waiting to drive me home again. I knew it looked bad and might prevent them from believing that this man was forcing himself on me and had been traumatising me since I was a little girl. And if they believed that I had lied about everything they would stop me from getting my kids back. That's how I felt anyway.

At some point I was allowed to take the kids out by myself. McDarby gave me some money and I brought them to the shopping centre in Dundalk. I had enough to buy them ice-cream and to let them go on the little rides in the mall. I did my best to make it seem like a happy day out for us, but inside I was dying of guilt and shame. I also visited them in their foster home, but only once or twice because I felt the foster parents disapproved of me as an unmarried mother. Then McDarby wanted to see them, claiming that he cared about him. The social workers didn't want him near the kids, but they didn't organise a barring or a protection order. I was simply told to tell him that he wasn't to go near them. It was confusing, since they had also written to him, to invite him in to talk about the children. I did my best to put him off, telling him that he wasn't allowed to see them. I also added that if he did see them it might affect me getting them back, but it made no difference. He insisted on coming with me to Dundalk, but agreed to sit at a distance away from us. However Ashley recognised him and told the social workers that she saw her Daddy, but that he hadn't come near her or Iseult.

He wanted the kids out of foster care, but not because he cared for them. He blamed the entire situation on my mother and brother, actually saying to Rikki, 'You put my children in care!' Yet when they were in Ardee, and I was in America, he never looked after them in any way. He only wanted them back because they were his possessions. The man was extremely possessive of his belongings. For instance his motorbike lived in the kitchen in Ardee and nobody was allowed to touch it. It didn't matter if it was in anyone's way, it could not be moved and that was that. He spent huge sums of money building up a collection of classic cars, but he never once allowed Rikki to drive one and never gave him a car. Like his cars, which he bought and then took apart, leaving their insides all over the house, the kids and I were just things to him, possessions to own and maintain control over.

The baby in my womb was further proof that I was weak and could not stop this man from abusing me. I was so ashamed and took no relief in the fact that the story, or bits of it, was out there now. I was mortified that people knew what he had done to me. I had let everyone down. I had allowed myself to be raped and now I had let the cat out of the bag. I could not be trusted. I felt I had caused all this trouble around me just because I couldn't stop that man from doing what he wanted to me whenever he liked. What was wrong with me?

It was beyond a nightmare because at least you can wake up from a nightmare. I felt I was existing in the centre of a volcano whose walls were on fire while below me was a deep crater filled with boiling lava. Since the top of the volcano was too high up for me to climb out of, I was well and truly stuck. On top of everything else I was suffering from bad headaches, brought on by stress no doubt.

The house in Ardee was a mess. The oil burner was now broken so it was always cold, while the rooms were full to the brim with bits of engines and junk. The kitchen floor was covered in oil and grease and Rikki's room was crammed with machinery of all kinds. McDarby's stuff had invaded the entire house and I had no energy to tackle the dirt or anything else. The entire place reeked of old alcohol and engines. There was never any food and yet there were mouse droppings everywhere. The only room that was relatively decent was the front room, so that anyone who dared to visit could believe that they had walked into a luxury home. Every day I'd light a fire and sit in front of the television with hardly a clue what programme I was watching. I did nothing else apart from visiting the kids when I could. My bump got bigger and I ate less; same old, same old. The social workers had said that the Ardee house was unsuitable for the children so I assumed I had to get another one, but how was

I going to get a house when I did not have a single penny to my name? I was like a three-year-old at a twenty-first birthday party; I simply could not make sense of what I was to do next.

Throughout all this he continued to rape me, maybe not as much as usual, but the threat was constantly there. Visits to the bathroom had to be kept as short as possible. There was no lock on the door and he would just come in on top of me. How I hated that cold dark room. Tiles were missing from the floor and there was no shower, just the bath that my father had put in. I was as terrified of McDarby as I always was. He only had to raise an eyebrow or lift his fist, ever so slightly, and I would begin to tremble. He had trained me to the point where my fear of him disabled me. I could do nothing to help myself against him.

When Christmas came round I packed up two black sacks of toys for the kids after scrounging some money from McDarby. I chose stuff like little teddy bears and dollies, stuff that I wanted to play with myself. I was seven months pregnant now, but was still able to conceal the bump beneath baggy clothes. Walking was difficult, but I was determined to show my kids that I cared about them. Nobody would give me a lift to Dundalk so I took the train. I was meeting the children in the social workers' office. My back was in agony, the sweat ran down my face and I had a stitch from the walk to the station, but it was worth it. I cried as the girls opened their gifts.

I was about seven months gone when I told him about the latest pregnancy. His response was to rent me a flat in Cabra. I have absolutely no memory of this flat only that when Megan was born in February, she slept in a drawer because I had nowhere else to put her. I remember sensing that he was pleased with this pregnancy as he thought it might confirm to the social workers that he was right in describing his sexual relationship with me as consensual.

Over the course of my sessions in the Rape Crisis Centre I did tell my counsellor about the abuse. I would have chosen my words carefully, but I did say I had first been abused when I was eleven years old, first raped when I was thirteen and that I had been pregnant when I was doing my Leaving Certificate. I also explained my predicament in that I was completely dependent on him for money. Furthermore I told her about my mother's drinking. It certainly was a big moment for me when she responded by saying that yes, this was an extremely abusive situation. And, yes, she believed me.

About a month before Megan's birth in February 1989 Mary, my counsellor, remarked on my never taking my coat off. The heating was on and I would sit there and sweat. It was only then that I unbuttoned the coat to show her my eight-month bump. She gasped, 'Oh my God!' Her surprise was an indication that I hadn't quite come out and confessed that the abuse was still ongoing at this point.

Next I had to 'confess' the pregnancy to the social workers, or maybe it was Mary who told them. I don't remember much about this, but I did have to miss my February visit with the girls because their sister finally arrived on 11 February. By now maybe everyone guessed that the father was my stepfather.

Much later on, McDarby had to come in with me for a meeting in the RCC where I was to tell him what it was like to be abused by him. He only agreed to come in because I lied and said I was getting the kids back. In any case I was unable to say a word. Instead I curled up in the chair. I couldn't speak, he wouldn't speak and Mary had to give up on the idea. It was a disaster and didn't help me with my trust issues regarding the centre. The social workers also brought us in together to discuss the children, but it was useless. I said nothing in front of him and he wouldn't answer their questions beyond a word or two. The only outcome was that McDarby was told to stay away from the children. Why couldn't that also have applied to me? However, the truth is it would have been impossible for me to break the connection with him because I depended on him for everything. I don't think the social workers or anyone else truly appreciated the trap I was in.

My financial dependence on him made me feel trapped. I needed money for counselling (I had to pay for the services at the RCC), I needed money for the children, I needed money for public transport to see the girls and I needed money for clothes for myself. Mother wouldn't give me a penny so I was tightly bound to him in order to get the kids back. He would give me a few hundred after I explained what I needed it for. It was a ridiculous situation. The money mostly went on the children and the counselling. I had no friends to speak of so there was no temptation to use it for a night out. In fact I don't think I would have known how to spend it on myself aside from buying a few bits of clothing.

And I'm keen to make this point, that there was no shortage of money. Many people may well assume that this sort of situation only happens in certain areas.

Looking back I'm sure I was trying to compensate

to the girls for the mess I had made. I bought them lots of presents because it made the visits a bit easier, to sit and watch their excitement as they unwrapped the dolls and the books and then help them to play with them. It was easier than just sitting there trying to make up conversation or games to play in front of the social workers. Later on I had to visit them in their home of their foster family. They also watched how I interacted with the girls because they would have had to report back to the social workers.

I had Megan in Holles Street. Rory spent the week in Ardee. As usual McDarby drove me to the hospital and only stopped long enough for me to get out of the car. After that I was by myself. It was important to him that I use different hospitals to stop any medical staff from joining the dots. Labour was a little over three hours. I didn't have a name ready, but while I was in the hospital I heard someone talking about a television programme and I realised that it was 'The Thorn Birds'. They kept mentioning the name Megan so I went with that. We left the hospital three days later.

It never occurred to me to give her up for adoption. I mean, I hadn't actually wanted Andrew adopted ... that had just spiralled out of my control. Perhaps it was because Andrew had been taken from me that I never considered not keeping Megan. It irks me today that no social worker or RCC staff asked me how I was going to look after this latest baby and, certainly, my stepfather was never approached for his opinion or plan of action.

Mother only found out about her when she was a few months old. I had moved to Cabra just before the birth – although I have no clear memory of this time at all. The bits I do remember are about how little I had. There was no pram, no cot and the landlord/lady did not allow babies. So I had to keep the baby quiet all the time. Also, because I had no babysitter, she came everywhere with me, to visit her sisters and to the RCC and, as a result, I formed a strong bond with her. I know I did not go out much and only spoke to shop assistants when I was buying stuff. I was still convinced that someone was out to get me and would break into the flat to attack me and the baby. I lived in constant terror, which must be the reason that my memory has shut down on so much.

Aunt Josie visited a second time after I had Megan. When she discovered I had had a new baby she was aghast. 'Oh, my God! How are you going to cope?' Any time she referred to McDarby she would say, ' … that abomination of a man!' She was absolutely enraged at my mother, believing that Mother knew exactly what was going on. 'How can she let this continue?' Again, I had no answer to that. Josie accompanied me on one of my office visits and, I think, made her own enquiries as to what was going on. I don't know what she found out or if she discovered any new information at all. Most likely the social workers did not tell her much as they preferred to deal with just me. This was the last time that I ever saw her. Her health was starting to fail and she was quite elderly by then. I could not blame her for feeling overwhelmed by my situation. No doubt she felt she could do nothing substantial to help me.

I had to bring Megan everywhere with me and so I introduced her to her sisters in front of their social workers. They were so excited to see her and wanted to touch her tiny hands. It was noted that the girls were always happy to see me and sad to see me leave. My hard work was gradually paying off.

In order to do this book I was asked why Megan wasn't taken into care. It is something I have wondered about over the years. The only answer I can come up with is that I must have come across as a good mother. I must have passed some test in the midst of all the chaos and darkness.

Eighteen long months passed before I got the girls back from their foster home in August 1989. When it looked certain that they were being given back to me, I asked McDarby what I was going to do. There was no way the kids and I could live together in the Cabra flat. He told me that he would get a house and, in due course, he rented a house in Monksfield, Clondalkin, Dublin 22.

CHAPTER ELEVEN

I didn't like the house. It was quite stark and the surrounding walls weren't high enough, as far as I was concerned. I didn't feel safe there. There was some furniture, just the basics – tables and chairs. However the carpets caused me a lot of stress because they were cream coloured, so everything showed up on them. I spent a lot of hours cleaning them.

However, the children's social workers from Dundalk came out to inspect it and seemed happy enough with it.

So I eventually got the girls back. It was a huge achievement and one that I probably did not bother to congratulate myself on. In any case I was so relieved to have them back with me. Rory was with us too and, of course, there was baby Megan and I suppose I tried my best to keep everything in control. Nevertheless, with them gathered around me, I discovered that I missed Andrew dreadfully. Now that I had all my children in the one place I could not forget that I had let him go. Ashley was old enough to miss him too and she asked where he had gone. That whole episode was pretty abstract in my mind and I replayed it over and over again, wondering how I had allowed him to be taken from me. I deeply regretted the adoption and still do to this day. All I could do was focus on his sisters and brother. I dared to dream that things might be different now and that I would find some way to keep McDarby out of our lives. I rarely visited Ardee now. My mother's screaming and abuse was too much for me to deal with. Typically, her response to Megan was to call her 'another of my husband's bastards!'

I threw out all the clothes that the girls had worn while in care, as part of my desire to put that awful time behind me. It took a while for them to settle back into living with me. I remember wishing I was more affectionate with them and longed to be able to hug and kiss them freely as I imagined other mothers doing, but, of course, I was still being abused, so it was unfair of me to expect that I could suddenly start behaving differently with them. I did strive to hug them, but there was little laughter in the house. I went through my day with one ear cocked for the sound of his car in the driveway. It was a horrible way to live. However, one thing that I was determined to do, but struggled with, was to read them bedtime stories. I'm not sure why I found that so hard to do. I could not have put on funny voices and I was unable to escape into those stories which were designed to reassure kids that things always worked out wonderfully in the end. I suppose I was still too stuck and traumatised.

We spent a year in that house and it is all a bit of a blur. I had to get the girls and Rory into school which then became part of my daily routine, walking them there and collecting them afterwards. When I approached the local school I had a bit of a panic. Naturally I did not want anybody knowing my story and I was convinced that people would look down on me because I had had all these children so close together and no wedding ring on my finger. My solution was to tell the school that I was fostering the kids. It was the only way to avoid any shame or stigma.

Apart from that I cared for the baby, cleaned the house and attended my sessions at the centre. I didn't stop to think about my life or how I felt about it. I was still on autopilot, like a robot, just carrying out the daily chores because they needed to be done and there was no one else to do them. And, of course, I had to continue to try fighting him off. I tried threatening him with the social workers and the Rape Crisis Centre and while I think it gave him something to think about, ultimately it did not prevent me from being raped every few days. He never changed, but why would he; I was the one in therapy.

He paid all the bills though I think the social workers might have helped me to get set up the children's allowance.

At one of my sessions in the RCC Mary asked me to look around her room and choose the object that I thought most resembled me and how I felt about myself. I picked out the tiniest thing she had, proving to her how small and insignificant I felt in a world that continued to overwhelm me. One time a woman was brought in to give the clients hand massages. She tried to hold my hand and every muscle in my body tensed. I fought the urge to thump her in the face and had to tell her that I didn't want a massage. I did not want anyone touching me.

A year later he actually bought a house in Monksfield, just across the road from the rented one. My father's petrol station was sold around this time and he took my share and put it towards the house, making up the balance with a loan. When he told me he was going to buy it I did not have an opinion one way or another. It meant little to me as I felt that he owned everything else. I have vague memories of packing stuff up and carrying them over the road to the new place. I didn't think much of the area. It was in a heap thanks to the new houses that were under construction all around me. There was little else by way of distraction. The house was semi-detached and a bit rundown, but he liked it because it had a proper garage. In other words he could drive into it and nobody could see him get out of the car.

Nothing in my immediate life had really changed. It was almost like my brief escape to America had never happened. Here I was back to looking after the children, hours upon hours of housework and having to deal with his frequent visits. The only difference was my dealings with the social workers and the Rape Crisis Centre. The children's social workers only visited me once or twice over the two years, which is surprising since Iseult and Ashley were still under the care of the health board. When they did visit it was primarily to inspect me and the home I was providing. As far as I could see, there was little curiosity about the father and neither did they ask who was paying the bills or how I was providing the food.

I had made no friends and felt completely cut off from the rest of the world and normal living. The usual rule applied: I wasn't to tell anybody about anything, so I kept myself to myself. This became a bit of a problem when the kids started to befriend other kids on our small estate. It was like we were slipping into a 'normal' life with the neighbours, but one I was ill equipped for. McDarby called in about four times a week and it cannot have escaped people's notice that he was much older than I was. I felt trapped all over again. I might as well have been back in Castleknock and began to long for some sort of support or maybe some way to escape my life again. Fortunately it was around this time, at the RCC, that I did begin to get to know other people through the workshops that I was obliged to participate in.

One friendly guy, who attended the RCC, struck up a conversation with me in the coffee room. Ben asked me my name and also if I had any children. I explained I did as a result of my abuse and he nodded, saying that he had heard about me. This was an unpleasant shock as it meant that somebody from one of the workshops I had done must have been talking out of turn, which was not allowed. I had a bit of a moment where I thought I was right not to trust anybody, and that people didn't care about me, they only wanted to gossip about my situation. When I calmed down, Ben and I discovered that we lived in walking distance of one another and he suggested that I call over for tea sometime. I also befriended a couple of women, too, though I would not have been overly chatty with them. Some of the group sessions were really tough and I would find myself slightly bewildered at the end of these sessions, when the group would bring out their guitars and sing as if they were the happiest crew in the whole wide world. I just couldn't understand how they could act so happy, though I appreciate now that this was their way of releasing emotional energy. I would have needed to release too, but, of course, I had to rush home to my children.

I found it difficult to truly connect with the other clients. This is a hard thing to admit to, but I know I would have been wholly conscious of the fact that nobody else had experienced the same level of continuous abuse.

People's reactions to my story were mixed. I kept expecting someone to shout and rant and do something – like call the gardaí – anything that would stop McDarby from attacking me. By this stage, lots of people knew about my situation: the social workers, the RCC and the friends I had recently made in there and even one or two of my neighbours. The responses were muted. Perhaps it was just too big a story for *normal* people to digest. Didn't the social workers say my whole situation was 'unbelievable', in other words echoing my rapist when he assured me that no one else would ever believe me?

But then there came a big, appropriate reaction which almost got me killed. I had gone to a New Year's party in a neighbour's house, two doors down, and McDarby showed up to demand that I come home. In other words, I was already in trouble for not being there when he arrived. The neighbour, a woman whose kids played with mine, and who I had briefly filled in about him, at once confronted him. Actually, she exploded at the sight of him, about his raping me and being my stepfather. 'Who do you think you are to treat her like that – you should be locked up because you are a sick man!' I froze and only moved to leave when he glared at me.

I hurriedly exited her house with him right behind me, but, to my utter horror, she pursued us, still shouting that there was something very wrong with him. When I got in our front door he snarled through gritted teeth, 'Get up them fucking stairs!' I obeyed, but he wasn't fast enough in locking the front door. He came up the stairs after me and all of a sudden the neighbour was there, on the landing, still hurling abuse at McDarby. I was terrified and wished she would disappear as I knew she was inadvertently earning me a hiding. Yet I admired her strength as she declared, 'You are a sick, perverted bastard!' I had never seen someone talk like this to him before. He lost his cool with her, something he never did so she must have rattled him, but he did his best to hide it, sneering at her that she was only a whore and a tramp. They were his favourite words. Not surprisingly the children woke up and I had to go in to settle them. Finally, she ran out of rage and stormed out of the house. Now he could punish me for her outburst. 'What are you telling people? How dare that tramp speak to me like that?' He flung me on the bed and, in between thumping me, he tried to strangle me. The violence was so sickening familiar that I found myself, in the middle of the attack, longing for a change. I mean that I wanted to die; I wanted him to finally make good on his threat. I wished for death because I suddenly realised that however much I tried to be a better person and a better mother it was all for nothing ,because I would always be his victim. So, really, what was the point of anything anymore? My eyes were bulging, my throat began to close over and I felt like I was being slowly buried beneath a dark, heavy blanket. I remember thinking that this was it and, at some point, I passed out. To my dismay I woke up the next day. For the following week I had to wear a scarf to hide the purplish imprints of his fingers. As much as I was glad to see someone going at him like that, I never spoke to my neighbour again – for my own safety.

Sometime after this I took Ben, from the RCC, up on his offer of a cup of tea. I had to put some planning into it since my life did not allow for any spontaneity. If I wasn't at the house when McDarby visited I was beaten up and also I had to collect the kids from school. Now, it wasn't that I particularly wanted to spend time with this guy, but I needed something different in my life. I needed to break the pattern of housework and abuse and find some space, however small, for myself to breathe in. A part of me had decided that this visit was going to happen, *had* to happen for my own sake.

I think I also wondered if Ben could help me. That need for help was motivating most of my actions at that point. It certainly was not a date. He just seemed like a nice person and I liked talking to him. Also he showed himself to be genuinely interested in the emotional welfare of my children and asked about them quite frequently. So, the big day arrived. His address was written down on a piece of paper that I had clenched in my hand and I couldn't quite believe that I was going to call upon him. I literally stayed long enough for one cup of tea mid-afternoon because it was too dangerous otherwise. He hadn't a clue that my abuser was still visiting me because I was afraid that he might mention it at the RCC. When I was leaving he asked if I would like to come again because he was having some friends over for dinner. This presented an enormous challenge to me because it would mean trying to leave the house at dinner time – obviously enough – and have the kids minded. However I just nodded and told him that I would think about it.

I had never gone to dinner in someone's house before and marvelled that this guy would make dinner for his friends. I did go, but only stayed for thirty minutes, if even that. It was more important that I follow through on my decision to do something for myself. Racked with nerves, I marched myself to his front door and knocked, hoping that he hadn't told his friends *all* about me. Couldn't I be just plain old Mary as opposed to Mary who has had all this shit in her life? That was an extra worry on top of my shyness and the fear of getting caught by McDarby. He was back at the house with the kids. I had told him I was running to the shops for beans or something so I didn't have much time to socialise.

There were two girls and another guy inside. I felt the usual panic about what I was going to say to them and took my chair in silence. They had finished their dinner by now which was fine by me as I was still barely eating and had no appetite from one day to the next. They were in fine form, all laughing and joking together. I felt a growing impatience as I watched the minutes ticked by. I accepted a cup of tea while the guy sitting opposite me, who introduced himself as Karl, sought to bring me into the conversation. He could not keep his eyes off me which made me uncomfortable plus he kept twiddling with his ponytail. It seemed that he did know a little about me and was bold enough to ask about my stepfather and money which I did not appreciate. I answered him rather sharply and turned away, deciding I did not want to talk to him, and just listened to the others. One of the girls, Jill, asked me for my phone number and I gave it to her because she was quieter than the rest.

The following week I met my host in the centre. He asked if he could visit me and the kids, but that would have been far too risky so I put him off. However, his friend called, the girl I gave my number to, and she came out and met the girls and Rory. I was slightly dismissive of her because her life experience was so far removed from mine, not that she knew that. I did not tell her much about me while she wanted to talk about boys and nights out. Apart from the abuse, I was a single mother with four young children who had no time to daydream about such unimportant things. Like the others I had met, she had no children. Therefore she was free to get a job and sit in people's houses, enjoying copious cups of tea and dinners. I envied her for that which is surely only natural. Nevertheless, whenever she asked me to meet her for coffee or to go window shopping I said yes whenever possible. I began to use the Rape Crisis Centre for practical purposes. I would tell McDarby that I had to go there for a workshop and he was bound to let me go since Iseult and Ashley were still Wards of Court.

One time she met me after my counselling session and invited me to meet the others for a coffee in Bewley's Café, George's Street, but the children needed to be collected from school. As usual I had Megan with me and I decided that the only way I could go to Bewley's would be if I got a taxi home afterwards, thus giving myself about forty or fifty minutes free time. Again I was acknowledging this new need to be around other people and do something different. I'll never forget the noise in the café. It was packed and I had to keep a grip on my panic as I searched for my friends. When I saw them and joined them at the table I immediately grew anxious about how I was going to contribute to the conversation. I was still struggling with my social skills.

These meetings in cafés became a lifeline for me. Otherwise my days were made up of getting the kids up, putting on their uniforms, making their lunches, feeding Megan and keeping the house really, really clean, and then collecting the kids from school, making their dinner and letting them play outside until evening, bringing them in and putting them to bed. Something had changed inside me; thanks to the Rape Crisis Centre I could no longer do without some form of a social life.

And, as it turned out, I made lifelong friends. Ben was not pretending to be concerned about my children; he was absolutely genuine. He knew that my kids were short on doting relatives so he took on the role himself, and, without fail, from that day forward he sends a Christmas box for the kids with the express instruction that it cannot be opened before midday on Christmas Day. As you can imagine, this caused the utmost excitement when the kids were young. Now, he wasn't wealthy and the gifts were usually small, but because of the way he presented them, in a big box, in which each gift had to be found amongst the straw he filled it with, the kids were never disappointed. Today he remains an important person in each of their lives and it all began back then in the RCC.

One afternoon I went into Bewley's and recognised the guy, Karl, with the ponytail and cheeky attitude. This time I allowed him to talk to me although I did not say much. Afterwards he asked for my number. Grudgingly I admitted to myself that I found him attractive, but I still was not impressed with his manner. In any case when he asked me out I agreed. In fact we met up again every day for the next two weeks. Because of my restrictions we met while the children were in school and Megan came everywhere with us. We went to another café on George's Street and, once or twice, we went as far as the cinema complex at the Square shopping centre in Tallaght.

He did most of the talking and these 'dates' could last no more than three hours or so. When I did talk, it was to create a fantasy life for myself … and him. Karl was trying to get to know me which meant asking me questions. Now he knew that I had been abused by my stepfather and that my children were his, so I could not make that disappear. However, I pretended that my real father was alive and was an extremely wealthy man who owned houses all over the world. Money would have helped free me from my stepfather. Besides, I did not want him or anybody else knowing that I was obliged to rely on my abuser for financial assistance.

At the cinema he encouraged Megan to throw popcorn on the floor. I thought this was absolutely appalling behaviour. He also got her to stamp about in puddles, something I would never consider doing. This was the carefree fun element that I knew I lacked as a mother and it threw me.

Group sessions at the RCC usually ran in the evening from 7 to 10pm and, whenever I could, I went along. Frequently the others went out together after-wards, but I wasn't always tempted to join them. They mostly talked about themselves and their lives and I could not afford to do that. Nobody knew I was finan-cially dependent on my abuser and still his victim. One of the few times I went along, Karl was there and the time had slipped by without my noticing it. When Karl told me it was almost 11pm I knew I was in serious trouble. Liam, a friend of his, offered to drive us both home. I did my best to hide my anxiety and was in the middle of asking the friend to pull over at the top of my road when McDarby's jeep shot by us. I had a panic attack there and then. I could not stop shaking and was hyperventilating, and then I actually threw up. It was like I was being chased down a street, but I was sitting still. That is the only way I can describe it. A voice was screaming in my head, 'What am I going to do? What am I going to do?'

Naturally the other two were bewildered by my behaviour. Eventually I told Karl that my stepfather was still around and that he refused to leave me alone. That was all I could say, but I think he was able to read between the lines and I was consumed with shame.

Liam begged me to come back to his house so that his wife could look after me. Because I did not know what else to do, I said yes, petrified that McDarby had seen me and would now follow us back to Tallaght. It all gets a bit blurry again. I think I stayed there a couple of nights out of sheer terror. Siobhan, Liam's wife, tried to get me to eat, but I couldn't and neither could I sleep out of worry for the children. Karl's friend drove me by the house and McDarby's jeep was there so I knew he hadn't abandoned the children.

McDarby got hold of the phone number for one of the girls from the RCC or maybe he found out where she worked and turned up, asking about me. I was told he was on the rampage looking for me. I don't know how many times I vomited over those couple of days. Siobhan suggested I get a barring order against him, but because I wasn't married I could only get a protection order. I honestly do not remember much about this beyond the fact that I had to fill out a form and tell whoever that my stepfather was abusing me. Siobhan accompanied me to the family law court in Dublin and I have drawn a complete blank about that experience because I was in such a state. It was her and Karl who kept reassuring me that I would be alright once I got the order, but I had little faith in it, believing that nothing could keep me safe from him.

Nobody official ever suggested that I take this route and get a protection order. This is what struck me at the time – why was it ordinary people who advised me on getting one and helped me with the application. This was the sort of help I had been for longing for from the social workers, something concrete.

I had to wait a few days for the order to go through and stayed in Karl's place, worrying myself sick over the children. McDarby was looking after them, but were they okay? Was he bringing them to school? Would he let them be taken into care again? The girls were still under a care order so perhaps this was not the best time to be doing this. I was plagued with self-doubt and could not understand Karl's confidence that it would all work out for the best. I felt I was looking down at myself and wondering what the hell I was doing. Did I have a plan? I was the mother of those children and I was McDarby's victim and there was a routine to this, a system. What would be the consequence of my breaking the system? I did not understand how my friends could be at all positive. All these people were involved in my life, but none of them had kids and neither did they have the faintest idea what McDarby was like. Only I knew how bad this could get.

When the order came through Karl accompanied me back, but I begged him to wait up the road until McDarby left. As soon as my stepfather saw me he threatened me about the protection order and told me that it would make no difference to him since there was more than one way of 'getting' me. And I believed him. He tore out of the house leaving me shaken and nauseous. Seconds later Karl was at the door, still adamant that everything was going to be better now. When he saw my terror he offered to stay with me to prevent McDarby from coming back and attacking me. Karl was smaller and slighter than McDarby and while I had no faith in him physically protecting me from my stepfather, he was the first person who had ever offered to defend me from being hurt. At long last I had found a true ally. And so he stayed with me, and no doubt had absolutely no idea what he was getting himself into. At just twenty-six years of age Karl took on a massive role without a moment's hesitation.

I learned that Karl was somebody who liked to take on causes and, initially, I felt that is all the kids and I were to him, people who needed his help. He immersed himself in our troubles and was much concerned with our welfare. Besides all that, he did his best to make me smile and even laugh though I was much too controlled to allow myself to laugh out loud. Getting involved with him was not an easy decision since I had McDarby's voice in my head telling me I was too ugly for anyone. If nothing else, getting involved with me was going to teach Karl patience, because he had to be patient on every level when it came to our budding relationship. In any case, we were both drawn to one another and this relationship began to flower in the middle of terror and utter chaos.

As a result of the protection order, McDarby withdrew all financial assistance. I did not have a penny to my name. I did not have a bank account and I had never paid a bill in my life. The ESB bill came in. I was in arrears and had ten days to pay it. By this stage Karl was opening the letters and trying to tell me not to worry. He was in college and also had a part-time job. When he could not be in the house he arranged for another friend of ours to sit with me. I was scared that McDarby would turn up, and grateful for the company.

McDarby began ringing the house and, when he was there, Karl would answer the phone to him. McDarby demanded to know what he was doing in his house and told him that he had better leave immediately. Karl would tell him, in turn, where to go and put down the phone. This went on and on with McDarby getting increasingly more abusive to Karl, but also asking him what he saw in me, as if I was a bit of dirt on the ground. Karl was genuinely bewildered that nobody had tried to stop this man from hurting me. Not once did it occur to me to have the phone number changed. As the phone calls came more and more frequently Karl's response was to tell the kids that they were going to have a screaming competition and so, when I was trying to listen to McDarby's threats, the kids were screaming their heads off. I could not understand Karl's attitude, but then again he could not have understood my terror. He did remark, however, on my controlling behaviour towards the kids. One evening he witnessed Rory, Ashley and Iseult line up at my side to have their homework signed by me. They presented their journals one after the other, in silence, and I never said a word to any of them, just signed my name and moved to the next one.

I had no money, and, for all their good intentions, Karl and our friends did not seem to realise the dire situation of being penniless, living in McDarby's house and having to feed four children. It was a genuine house of cards in that I felt that it could not last. I needed money. *I needed money*. When McDarby rang and said that he would give me money, but only if I met him up the hill from Monksfield, I said yes. And that was inevitable. He parked up the hill and as soon as I opened the passenger door he told me to get Karl out of his house or else. I climbed in and said nothing, desperate not to provoke him into wanting to confront Karl at the house. I went along with everything because it was the only option I had. I allowed him to think that I would obey him and get rid of Karl. He handed me the money with a smug expression on his face. 'See', he said, 'You have nobody else to help you except me, but if you keep me from my house and kids that will be the end of it. You will have absolutely nothing then.' I hated having to sit there like a beggar waiting for my handout.

Well-meaning people kept telling me that I just had to keep him away, but I did not know how to do that. That man had controlled me – body and soul – for over ten years now and I was not equipped to make a final break because I could not live without his money to feed the children and pay the bills. And nobody seemed to be able to conjure up a better alternative than McDarby in that respect. He paid the mortgage and all the bills and bought all the food and all the clothes and all the shoes and all my counselling. Tell me, how I was to suddenly let go of that?

In spite of the protection order he turned up at the house once or twice and Karl called the guards. I felt my world was crashing down around my ankles. And I suppose in a way it was. Karl represented a massive change, a whole new order to how I had been used to living my life. I could not catch up with myself. It was difficult enough for me to enter into a relationship and try to find some semblance of normality. Karl could have sex with me, but he could not get near me mentally or emotionally. Thanks to my stepfather I was indifferent to the sexual act. There was no kissing; it was simply a matter of 'insert here'. Neither could he hug me, but I would let him hold my hand for all of ten seconds before it became too much. Intimacy was an alien concept to me. Of course he saw that I switched myself off in bed. He wondered was something wrong between us, but I had no answer for him; there was a lot that Karl still didn't know, not least about Andrew's adoption. I had no idea how to be in a relationship with anyone. When I had time to think about all that was going on, I only felt guilty and anxious about Karl getting involved with me and my mess. He was being enmeshed in this sickness that was my life, and it did not seem fair on him.

The situation was utterly chaotic and that is putting it nicely. It did not occur to either of us to use contraception and a few months later I found myself pregnant again, but this time with Karl's baby.

CHAPTER TWELVE

This pregnancy was so different from the others. For one thing I had proper hospital appointments beforehand and, for another, Karl accompanied me to them. This time I had to hide my pregnancy from McDarby. Of course he found out and called me a whore, quickly following this up by saying that if I left Karl he would take the baby on as his.

Around this time my counsellor left the Rape Crisis Centre to set her up own practice, but I could not afford to continue seeing her as she had to charge more than I had been paying. In desperation, I went to a local doctor who put me in touch with a Holy Ghost father who worked as a psychotherapist, doing irrational and emotive therapy. Little did I know that I would have to meet with him for the next ten years. Nevertheless I liked the fact that he was a priest because I did worry that I was evil or possessed in some way. How else could I explain why this stuff happened to me?

McDarby demanded to see his children. In relation to Karl he would growl, 'I don't want any man near my children!' It was his way of trying to maintain control of me. He was trying to alter my feelings for Karl, making out that all men abused children and could not be trusted. I tried to put him off seeing the kids, but there were times that he refused to be thwarted. Because I did not want him near the house I brought the kids up the hill to meet him in his car. I was afraid they would blurt out about Karl still living in the house, but there was no way I was going to imitate my stepfather and tell my kids not to say this or that. He knew Karl was still around, but perhaps only thought that he visited the house. All I could do was hope that the subject did not come up. He gave them all a few pounds and the conversations were mercifully brief, but forced.

Karl was in college one day so my friend Jill was with me in the house. I remember saying, 'I just can't break free from him.' She floored me with her reply, 'Do you think you have a dependency on him?'

Her words affected me deeply because I had told myself that if I could just break the chain with McDarby then everything would be fine, but the truth was I had a huge dependency on him. It was like he had taken me hostage all these years and a part of me was absolutely entwined with him. He owned me and I was completely in tune with him. I could read his expression; I could guess his reaction to something; I could interpret a sentence from a single grunted word. It was a curse. I was cursed. Everyone else in my life, aside from the kids, seemed so different and new. I struggled to gauge responses to my few friends, Karl and my therapist. I struggled to know them and find my role in relation to them. I kept feeling they never really and truly understood my life. It was so easy for everyone to tell me not to go see McDarby, but they had little idea of the terror I experienced if I didn't.

There were problems that I could not have foreseen. Rory, who was about ten or eleven at this time, asked me why Daddy wasn't coming around anymore. I had not realised that he knew McDarby was his father; that is, I hadn't realised that he had fully understood the situation. He and I had never discussed it and I certainly never ever imagined that he might want to spend time with his father. It honestly came as a bit of a shock to me. Now, when McDarby rang he asked to speak to his son, and only later I discovered that he was urging Rory to tell Karl to get out of his daddy's house and not to listen to Karl because he had no rights over him. Naturally this resulted in Rory not liking Karl.

To my surprise Karl wanted to be with me in the Coombe for the birth. When I asked him why, he replied, 'Because it's my baby too!' I found it peculiar and did not quite trust him yet. I did not really believe that he wanted to be there because he cared for me. There was just so much awfulness going on and I was still holding him at a distance, along with the rest of it. I remember one time he placed his hand against my cheek and I burst into tears. It was hard to deal with such gentleness and I retreated inside myself.

When Dillon was born, Karl was so excited. His name was a result of my being a huge Bob Dylan fan. I am still a fan today, although some of his sadder songs can still affect me today. Karl bought me flowers, which made me cry because this had never happened before. Meanwhile, I was also afraid because I was bringing his son into McDarby's house. It was such a bewildering experience. People were happy for me and my new baby. People we knew bought him presents and wanted to hold him. When I brought him to the shops, people would peer into the buggy and tell me he was gorgeous. Imagine this: this was my fifth baby and I had never experienced any of this before. So, this was what being 'normal' was like.

I tried my best, I really did, but I was not coping after Dillon's birth. McDarby continued to ring the house to issue his usual threats and abuse, and I would go to meet him to keep him away, as I was sure that he would try to kill Karl if he got close enough. The house was too small for all of us and Rory wanted to see his father. Having a baby with someone who cared for me was exploding walls I was desperately trying to hold on to. When Dillon was just a few months old I told Karl that he would have to take the baby and leave. Once more I was beginning to fall apart. McDarby was withholding money again and, in my damaged head, all I could think to do was return to what I knew. Therefore, the newest additions to the house – Karl and Dillon – would have to leave. When Karl refused to go I panicked. Fortunately he recognised that I needed help, so he approached the public health nurse for home help which duly arrived in the shape of a lovely, warm lady called Kay. Through her, Karl got in touch with the wonderful Carmel M, who was a social worker with the health board. An older woman, she was genuinely caring and supportive of us. It was thanks to her that we started talking about going to the guards so that I could make a statement against McDarby, whose response to Dillon's birth was typical, 'Oh, another bastard!'

I dreaded the thought of going to the guards, but Carmel and Jill came with me. I had no idea what to expect and was shocked to discover that the gardaí needed facts about every single thing that I wanted to put into my statement. Therefore I was obliged to go back over my entire story and provide details like the locations and dates of the attacks. Because I was dealing with years of abuse, I had to visit the station every day, for several hours, for months on end. A friendly male detective and a female garda were put on my case. They picked me up at the house and drove me there and home again. What kept me going throughout all this was the belief that McDarby would finally be stopped from hurting me. I absolutely believed that this would work, that McDarby would be arrested and charged with statutory rape, that the justice system would be my saviour. Also, I just wanted my life validated: this is what happened to me and here is the evidence.

My stepfather was upping his financial advantage. If I told him that I needed four hundred pounds he would give me a hundred and say that he'd have the rest in a few days, but then he would eke out the balance, making sure that it was necessary for me to go meet with him again and again. It was his way of retaining control of me.

The gardaí were shocked by my story, frequently exclaiming, 'Oh my God!' I told them everything, about how Dad died and then McDarby's moving in with us and so on. Rory and I had to have a blood sample taken to prove that I was his mother and that he was the age he was. In other words they could confirm that I had become pregnant when I was sixteen and had him when I was seventeen. Now they could get McDarby on statutory rape since the legal age of consent in Ireland was seventeen years. I found it extremely stressful. Despite having been at the RCC, this was the first time that I had discussed the abuse in such great detail and with gardaí too. I had to relive stuff I wanted to forget and I became paranoid that McDarby would discover what I was up to. Surely he would see in my face that I was telling on him.

This is going to sound preposterous, but during all of this McDarby seemed to notice that I was stressed and he decided it was 'that Karl' that was causing it, so he set about organising a holiday for us to give me a break from Karl.

Yes.

I know.

He took me and the kids on a four-day trip to a themepark in Wales. I remember very little about it, but I think the kids enjoyed themselves. Why did I agree to go? I was so obsessed with him suspecting me of talking to the guards that I seized this as an opportunity to keep him happy. I thought, 'if I do this he'll definitely never guess that what I am up to.' I found a local babysitter and brought her with us because I did not want to be alone with just him and the kids. And that trip is one of my biggest regrets today, but I can see why I went through with it. I was keeping the peace and behaving 'normally' as best I could.

However, I could not tell the friendly gardaí where I was going and Karl struggled to follow my line of reasoning. He knew I was not in a good place because of the statement and he did his best to accommodate the madness. I knew that no one would understand it. It was four days of intense acting on my part. I felt McDarby could read me as well as I could read him so I had to pretend everything was as it should be, while inside I was getting more and more hysterical. Looking back, I don't think I said more than a handful of words during the trip because I was trying to keep myself intact. I made sure that the babysitter, the kids and I slept in the same room.

On my return, Karl told me that he had watched a documentary on the Stockholm syndrome and felt he was only now beginning to appreciate the effect that a lifetime of abuse had on me, how I felt so caught up in my stepfather even after all he had done to me. I listened to him, longing to understand myself while I felt so guilty about getting McDarby into trouble. The name came from a Stockholm bank robbery in 1973 where a robber took four hostages and over the course of six days a relationship developed between the captor and his captives to the extent that one of the female hostages wanted to leave with him and there were false rumours of an engagement. The captor had found himself unable to kill the hostages and blamed them for being too friendly to him, while they had begun to think of him as their leader, someone who should be praised for not hurting them more. In fact the hostages became anxious that it would be the police who would hurt and even kill them while they continually used the adjective 'kind' to describe their captor. It is a defence mechanism and occurs in situations where a person is physically threatened by a captor or abuser and firmly believes that their life is in danger. The dominant perception of their situation is their captor's/abuser's perception and they absolutely believe that it is impossible to escape their tormentor, in that they feel bound to him as much as they fear him. Sound familiar? Possibly what was most difficult to understand for the people who came into my life, including the social workers and solicitors, was the fact that I truly believed my life was in danger from this man.

The weeks passed as I waited and waited to hear about the case. I was stuck in limbo. The idea of standing up in a courtroom terrified me, but I thought I might just be able to do that if it meant an end to the violence and rapes. And then one day the phone rang. I answered it and it was my stepfather proudly informing me that he was not going to be prosecuted. With all that I have forgotten, his exact words that day will never leave me: 'I told you that nobody would believe you. You're only a mouth!' Ireland and the Office of the Director of Public Prosecutions (DPP) had failed me. My stomach sank, my blood ran cold. For that horrendous moment, I was stunned.

I cannot say that my life fell apart at this point because it was already in a million pieces, but it certainly felt like an extra layer of darkness had descended. How was this possible? I had found the courage to go to the guards and took months to make a statement, helped by sympathetic reactions from the detective and the garda who had dealt with me, not to mention the social worker and all the friends I had told my story to, or at least, bits of my story. I think Karl was the only person who was witnessing my entire story at first-hand and learning about the different sides to me. How was it possible that someone sitting in an office could read the facts and decide against a court case? Karl went mad and began a campaign of phone calls to anyone he could think of. He just refused to accept the news and wrote to the DPP's office, demanding an explanation. He received a letter explaining that the DPP felt it would have been detrimental to my children to pursue the case. All I could think was that this was never ever going to stop. Nobody was going to stop McDarby from possessing me. Nobody.

Dillon was about six months old now and I did my best to block out the hurt and shock by focussing on him and the children. Possibly I was also suffering from post-natal depression, but I'm not sure. The months after this letdown are lost in a fog. I did go to my doctor, but refused his prescription for anti-depressants. I had no real understanding of depression back then and saw it as something shameful on top of all the other stuff. I felt it was bad enough that I needed home help. I saw it as a sign of weakness and did my best to tidy up before she arrived. In my mind if I could keep the house clean and tidy then I was showing the world that I was okay. I spent so much time worrying about what other people thought of me – the shame of my past, the sexual abuse – and the years of trying to hide it was demanding.

I was tired all the time. The housework and the parenting were overwhelming. Karl was in college so there was no wage coming in and the mortgage wasn't being paid. I saw my therapist twice a week and managed to scrape together the donation required. Because of the statement, McDarby withdrew all financial assistance and my life began to resemble a long, dark tunnel with no ending. I briefly thought about ending my life when the State refused to recognise my plight, but that would have required energy I did not have. At the same time, however, I did sort of give up on myself. One day I rang Carmel, the social worker, and asked her to visit me. The kitchen was in a heap and there were about twenty loads of washing sitting around the place waiting to be done, but I could do nothing. Gone were the days of my intense cleaning; these days I had no time, no energy and couldn't see the point in washing floors and walls. She suggested I needed a rest and that she would have the kids looked after. What she came up with was a temporary bed in St Loman's Hospital. She took charge because I was incapable of making any decisions and it was she who packed a small bag for me.

Since Karl was in college, and the kids were in school, she left a note for him explaining where I was going and then she drove me to the hospital. I had to sign myself in and was put under the care of a lovely doctor who told me that I shouldn't be there. However he also tried to give me anti-depressants, but I refused them. He told me something that I have never forgotten: 'Mary, mad people don't know that they are mad.'

Carmel split the kids up between various homes, but I was alright with that because I trusted her and I knew this was temporary. Because Karl and I weren't married, Dillon had to be sent off too. I was taken to a ward and given a bed. Unsure what to do next, I sat there and looked around me. A woman wearing a scarf danced around the ward oblivious to the rest of us. I could not take my eyes off her. There were all kinds of people in there with all kinds of problems. That evening I watched a line of patients take their medication. They opened their mouths and the pills were dropped inside. I had refused to take anything. As the hours passed I began to get more and more upset. What the fuck was I doing in here? I was not mad, the doctor had already said I shouldn't be there, but no one knew what else to do with me. So, here I was in a mental hospital while my violent rapist of a stepfather was out there walking around as free as a bird. I had done nothing wrong. I did not deserve this, but the DPP had shown me that McDarby was always going to be a free man, free from consequences and retribution. It was only me that had to suffer.

In fairness I felt this was an epiphany of sorts to know vehemently that I had done nothing wrong and that I did not *deserve* to be there. McDarby was the wrongdoer, not me.

To calm myself, I reasoned that once Karl read Carmel's note he would come to see me. I never doubted that for a second. I waited and waited until he finally arrived. As soon as I saw him I whispered, 'They're all mad in here. I can't stay, I have to go!' He looked at me as if to say, 'But you're in here so perhaps you are a bit mad too.' Shaking my head, I told him, 'No, Karl. I am not mad. I cannot stay here.' I asked about the kids and he assured me that they were grand. And then we planned our escape route. I gave him my little bag and walked him to the front door as if to say goodbye to him, only I kept walking. Once outside we broke into a run. At the end of the driveway, Karl flagged down a taxi. On the drive home

Karl told me that over the years he had met quite a few people who had had to visit relatives in mental institutions and the first thing that each and every patient ever said was, 'I'm not mad. You have to get me out of here!' On his way to visit me he had hoped I would not say the same thing.

When we got back to the empty house I saw the mess as if for the first time. Dirty plates, cups and laundry were all over the place. I sat down and began to fret about the hospital's reaction to my disappearance. I had visions of men in white coats pulling up and dragging me out to a van. It was best that we ring them and let them know where I was. Since the phone bill had not been paid in months we had to walk to Clondalkin village and ring from a payphone. Karl had to make the call for me. They hadn't yet realised I had escaped and tried to assure Karl that I was asleep in bed. It was decided that I would visit the day centre instead, which I did a few days later. Next we had to ring Carmel. It had been a big moment for me, to have been in that hospital and be absolutely sure that I did not belong there. There was a lot wrong with me, but I did not belong in a mental institution. That was good to know.

It took some time to get all the children back.

Carmel had decided I needed a break and that was what she had organised for me. Dillon came home first because he was a baby and had been staying just down the road from the house. Ashley and Iseult were in Madonna House, but at least I could get to them easily enough to see them and make sure they were okay. However Megan and Rory were with a foster family in Arklow and we didn't have any transport, so that was a problem. We rang them every day, but Megan wasn't coping. Her foster mother said she needed her eyes tested as she was stumbling all over the place. This didn't sound right to us and we asked Carmel to visit her. It turned out that Megan was suffering from separation anxiety: it was her first time away from home and me, and as a result, she stopped eating and drinking. She ended up in Cherry Orchard Hospital suffering from dehydration. A week later she was back home with us. In the meantime I continued to see my therapist and I made efforts to look after myself, even agreeing to take anti-depressants. Following six months of worry, and visiting the children as much as we could, they were finally back home with us.

Meanwhile Karl was still in a rage over what had happened with the DPP. He just would not let it go while my attitude was, in comparison, 'same shit different day'. What was the point of staying angry, nothing was going to change. I was still trying to get maintenance out of McDarby, but he was refusing to give me anything unless he was allowed to see the kids. Despite his doings he was legally entitled to see them because he was their father. However, after the allegations I had made against him, he had to be supervised for his visits, but there was nobody available to do this apart from me. Karl was, understandably, like a lunatic over this because he strongly felt that the man should not be allowed anywhere near children. It was Carmel who suggested to him that I take a civil action case against McDarby because that would mean he had to prove that he did not abuse me.

We were in a vulnerable position due to the fact that the house was in McDarby's name and the mortgage was being paid by him – or was meant to be paid by him at any rate. Letters arrived every day for McDarby and Karl eventually opened one of them to discover that the house was being repossessed. We had one month to find somewhere else to live. Karl got someone to drive him down to the bank's solicitor to explain the situation to them. He explained who exactly was living in the house, adding that it was my stepfather who owned it and that I was preparing a statement with the guards over years of abuse. When they continued to look unimpressed Karl threatened to go to the newspapers. I had no idea he was doing this. McDarby had told the solicitors that his other assets were a farm in Carlow and my mother's house in Ardee. Thanks to Karl we heard no more about the house being taken from us.

In the midst of all this Christmas was approaching. A solitary miniature tree was my only decoration and I put it on top of the television. When Karl saw it he was incredulous, asking me, 'Eh … is that it?' There had always been decent Christmas trees in Ardee, it was just everything else that was awful, and I had forgotten how to make an effort. Karl took the kids off and returned with the biggest tree I had ever seen. He struggled to get it through the front door and I was convinced it was a disaster, but he showed me how to celebrate Christmas by making the effort to put up a fabulous tree and then go to the bother of decorating it with lights and ornaments. I was the introvert, he was the extrovert, a little over the top, but the kids loved it. I remember thinking I was glad he was there to show them there was another way to be.

One day Karl told me he had found me a solicitor, a woman based in a practice in west Dublin. I did not like the sound of her. When Karl went to see her she abruptly cut him off and just said, 'Bring her in and we'll see what we can do.' I also found her abrupt in person when I went in to give her my permission to get my statement and anything else that was on file for me. However, when I met her the second time, she was much warmer, having read my file. I don't think she could quite believe the lack of responses from the various people who knew my story and she quickly compiled a list of names I should take action against, assuring me that I had a really strong case.

So this was going to be a bigger and broader step up from my previous effort solely to have my stepfather arrested and put away. This was a civil action case. She was going to pursue not just McDarby, but everyone who had let me down including a nominee of Our Lady of Lourdes Hospital, and of the Coombe Hospital, and of the National Maternity Hospital, Holles St, three doctors, an adoption society, the North Eastern Health Board, the South Western Health Board.

Another situation loomed at home. Twelve-year-old Rory was increasingly unhappy living with Karl and me. He had had a lot to deal with all his young life. The blood tests proved that McDarby was his father and, thanks to his father's manipulation, he could not accept Karl in the house. Of course his father was using him to create tension. McDarby would tell Rory ridiculous tales about Karl calling him names and making threats against him and, of course, he believed his father. It got to the stage where Rory hated Karl and was demanding to go and live with McDarby. I had no idea what to do until Carmel, the social worker, told me, 'Well, Mary, if that's what Rory wants to do, you just have to let him do it.' I thought she was crazy, but then she asked me if I thought that McDarby would take Rory in. I shook my head immediately and said 'No!', but how could I say this to my son. Rory packed one bag. I only found out afterwards that he told all his school friends that he was moving in with his Dad and would not be coming back ever again. Carmel drove the three of us to meet McDarby and, of course, McDarby refused to take him in. He spun Rory a story about not having a house for him and that he would have to build him one first. Of course I knew he had the houses in Carlow and in Ardee. His attitude was only what I had expected, but Rory was absolutely devastated.

It was suggested that he go into a therapeutic home where he would get help and support, and while it broke my heart, I felt I needed to let him go. However, like everything else in my life, this home provided further evidence of how the state and people in charge can let you down. It turned out that the home was faced with allegations that one of the staff was abusing the boys, but thankfully, nothing ever happened to Rory. In any case, it is Rory's own story to tell so I won't say any more about it.

The months went by and I continued with my visits both to my therapist and my solicitor. I was doing my best to be happy with what I had. I made a few more friends and all the while, thanks to Karl and these friends, I was learning how abnormal my previous life had been. I wanted desperately to succeed at this new life. I did not really 'do' happiness, but my anger was gone, or at least had diminished in size. Of course I had my dark days, but I did my best to keep them to myself as much as I could. The only times I saw McDarby were during his access visits with the kids in order to get money for them. Despite this he was still ever-present in my head. I did not have to be standing in front of him to be affected by him. The truth was that, aside from Rory, the kids did not want to see him. Iseult actually said she hated him and found him 'creepy'. She would start crying as soon as I said we were going to meet him. We usually met in the local branch of McDonald's. I never said much and just let him talk to the girls. I don't think he ever knew about the house being repossessed. I never wanted to go with the kids, but if I didn't turn up no money would be handed over. All he could do was ask how school was and then give them some money. It was horribly stilted and hardly lasted the hour before we all bolted in relief, glad the visit was over.

I discovered that nine-year-old Megan was being bullied by an older boy in the area. Carmel suggested that the girls might benefit by going into Rainbows group therapy. This service had been set up for children who had lost parents through death or separation. I wasn't convinced by this. Yes, my kids were separated from their father, but he was not a normal father to them and never had been. I felt the system lacked anything definite for someone in my situation and my children's. As far as I could see there was nothing in place for the likes of us in terms of support. Having said that, the girls enjoyed the project they went on and through them I learnt about this notion of pampering oneself. They had been taught to create space for themselves in order to do something nice, like light candles and take relaxing baths. Watching them learn about themselves and their bodies in a positive way was an eye-opening experience for me. Something was starting to awaken within me thanks to my daughters.

My solicitor had become my true knight in shining armour. There was a wonderful connection between us. Over the course of the last nine months I had come to trust her and believe that she was going to make the difference for me. It seemed so obvious now. What I had needed all along was a woman to fight for me and I began, for the first time ever, to allow myself to imagine that my journey to justice might be approaching its conclusion. One day she asked me to drop by. I went in and she led me to the chair in the office and sat me down, telling me that this was one of the hardest things that she had ever had to do. I felt suddenly fearful and then I heard her tell me that she was leaving the office to take another job elsewhere. I could not take it in. I may even have cried. She tried to reassure me that her boss, a male solicitor, was taking over my case and that he would take great care of me.

CHAPTER THIRTEEN

Karl had finished college and now had a part-time job, so he was able to help me more at home. I watched his naturalness with the kids and theirs with him and I badly wanted to be more relaxed in myself. He brought me out and about to different places to get me away from the house. I don't doubt that I looked, acted and sounded a lot older than I was and I craved to be able to let go. My life experience had been so narrow. I watched Karl in awe when he greeted other people as if he hadn't a care in the world. I was his complete opposite and would be self-conscious and embarrassed about admitting how many children I had, feeling sure that people were constantly judging me.

When my previous solicitor left the practice I had no choice but to believe that her boss would do his best by me. Things moved incredibly slowly and I would ring, from time to time, to see what was happening. Actually, it would be fairer to say that Karl would tell me to ring and I would have to steel myself to make the call. I found it intimidating to ring the office and told myself that he was the solicitor and, therefore, knew what he was doing. There was no need to worry or hassle him. I also had a couple of infrequent meetings with him, but nothing much was happening.

Rory made his confirmation in 1993. I got him his clothes and dressed myself for the occasion. Karl and I were there and, Jill, my friend, stood as his sponsor. A little while later I discovered I was pregnant again. I was determined to be 'normal'. I did struggle with it, but I decided that I had had enough of traipsing into hospitals. For this pregnancy I was going to attend my own doctor. I also decided that I had had enough of being an unmarried mother. This was my seventh pregnancy and I was done with snooty looks at the absence of a wedding ring. The kids were getting older and bringing friends into the house, which threw me, as I imagined that if their parents came in they would be able to see that our family was very different from theirs. I was tired of feeling ashamed of myself. I said as much to Karl who was only too happy to hear it. He seized the moment and got down on bended knee and proposed to me, presenting me with a ring he had bought weeks earlier.

From the beginning, this pregnancy felt different. I could even feel the baby moving around a lot earlier than the others. When I was thirty-three weeks gone

I told the doctor I was worried and he sent me for a scan. At the hospital I had a bit of a jolt. We found out we were having twins. Karl started laughing and was beside him with joy while I was crying, wondering how on earth I was going to cope with two babies.

Now that I had an engagement ring on my finger and the babies were on their way, I decided it was time for Karl to meet my mother. It was all part of this new normal life I was trying to create for myself. It was not an easy decision, but I wanted to show her that I had found someone, to see if it improved how she felt about me. For years she had blamed me for seducing my stepfather and called me horrible names. How she could still blind herself to the truth was beyond me. Surely, now that I had my own fiancé things could be better between us? But how was I going to do this? I dreaded Karl seeing the wreck of the house in Ardee. Also, I did not relish us turning up to find Mother incoherent with drink. I could phone her to tell her we were on our way and she might be sober then, but, in the time it would take us to reach Ardee, the situation might well be disastrous. And then there was McDarby. I absolutely did not want to see him nor oblige Karl to have to deal with him, but if I wanted this to happen then I was just going to have to face the risk of it being bloody dreadful.

So, we went. My stomach was knotted from fear and anxiety. The house resembled a junkyard, but Mother was sober when we arrived. However, I could see her sneaking vodka and after an hour I knew it was time to leave. We discussed the wedding and who I could invite from her side. As you can imagine, that was not an easy conversation. Nevertheless I hoped that I would have some family with me on my wedding day. We left before she got abusive, not that Karl knew that. On the way home he remarked that she seemed very nice. I said nothing, but was relieved, all the same, that it had gone as well as it did.

Karl organised the wedding. The only thing I had to do was get my dress, which presented its own difficulties as I could not stop feeling that this should be an enjoyable task to do with my mother. I had met his parents, but felt that my past was too much for them to deal with. I wished that my mother would have taken more of an interest in matters and helped me plan the wedding, but, as usual, she was too far gone to be of any help. I had never organised so much as a tea party in my life and Karl, seeing me waver under the pressure, took over the preparations himself. Our budget was tiny, so Karl had to be really inventive. Also, I had no one to give me away until Karl's father, Pat, agreed to do it. It saddened me that my own father wasn't there to do the job. My two brothers were dealing with their own issues arising from an alcoholic mother so I did not attempt to push them into a role that I guessed they were unable for. The one thing I made sure of was that McDarby would not be around.

Of course Mother told him about the wedding. He rang to give out to me, telling me that Karl was only after his house and my money. I wondered what money he meant exactly. He also assured me that I could not depend on Karl, who would surely leave me at some point.

While Karl was running around getting prices for flowers and so on, I was ringing the solicitor every now and then to see how the case was progressing. He was often too busy to talk to me so I would leave messages and get frustrated if he didn't call me back. When he did ring me it was to tell me that things were still progressing and that he would be serving papers *soon*. I was surprised at how slowly things were moving yet I had no reason to doubt him; he was my solicitor after all.

Aside from that, a different energy was coming in around me. I started going to a hairdresser up the road. I know you might struggle to understand how this was such a big deal for me, but it was. It was like I had been locked up since I was a child and now, with Karl in my life, I was able to try out things that were perfectly normal for everyone else. I found it bewildering to sit there and listen to the other women tell the hairdressers about their lives and their family. Why on earth did they want to do that? I could never imagine myself opening up like that.

The night before the wedding was a peculiar one for me and I found myself assailed by doubts and fears. I had time to dwell on the fact that I was ten months older than Karl and he was, in my opinion, much better-looking than me. I heard my stepfather's voice tell me over and over again that I was ugly, ugly, ugly. I fought demons that night and did my best to banish them by the time Jill, my good friend and bridesmaid, arrived the following morning. She blew away my fears as she agreed to wear make-up just for me and put on her lilac dress. Then she helped me to put on mine. My four-month bump was practically invisible under my dress.

Karl had organised a car to bring me and his father to the church. I was nervous and hoped that my mother was at the church and sober. I knew Rikki would be there because his friend was going to take the photographs. As soon as I got out of the car I searched for Rikki amongst the small crowd of well-wishers and mouthed to him, 'Is Mother here?' He shook his head and mouthed back, 'I'm sorry, Mary.' That was hard. It was only then I realised that I had actually believed she was going to make the effort and come to her only daughter's wedding. Now I had to keep smiling as I took Karl's father's arm and walk up that aisle, doing my best to hold back my tears of hurt and disappointment. In any case the service was lovely and I kept my own name, Manning, because it was the only thing left to me that belonged to my father.

Afterwards we went to the Springfield Hotel in Leixlip and I was touched to see my mother's sister and her husband turn up for the party, adding to the small number that were there for me, bringing it to a grand total of eight out of the eighty guests present. Again I was torn, enjoying the day while feeling sad about the huge spaces that I could not shrug off. Dad was gone, my stepfather was a rapist monster and my mother was a no-show. Nevertheless, I did manage to enjoy the day. Karl's parents gave us enough money to stay in a tiny, horrible room in Blackpool for our honeymoon. The kids were left in Rikki's tentative care while we took off for a few days. It was over before we knew it and we were back home, with me trying to get my head around the fact that two babies were arriving in the next five months.

The mean voice in my head told me: *this is it; this is your lot in life.* I was back to minding children and doing housework and it was consuming me. Somehow, in the midst of the exhaustion and routines, I felt that there was more to me than this. I was not yet done. Housework and childminding were not my sole reasons for being on this planet. I was still seeing my therapist twice a week and maybe he helped inspire me to think about opening my mind and myself up to new experiences. Karl had his part-time job and I began to think that I might do some kind of course.

The twins, Amber and Nathaniel, arrived on 6 March 1995, 6 lbs 3 and 6 lbs 4. I didn't have an epidural, but I got through it ... just about. Amber was delivered first and the labour was awful. I decided on her name after visiting the hospital, when I was thirty-three weeks pregnant, to discover I was having twins. Walking down the road in a daze, I had stopped at the traffic lights. I watched them change to amber and it suddenly struck me that the colour would make a beautiful name. During the labour on Amber

I decided that I had had enough pain for one day, thank you very much, and shut my body down. I was about seven centimetres dilated with another three to go when I informed the staff around me, 'No, I am not doing this!' I never raised my voice, I was simply informing them of my decision. Naturally the doctor, nurses and Karl began to beg me to keep going, please keep going! I shook my head and repeated what I had said. Then the doctor told me that he was worried that the baby might be breech. Somewhere deep inside me I heard a voice tell me to keep going. And so I did. Fortunately the second birth went much fast than the first one. Karl chose Nathaniel's name. He had always liked it and when he looked it up he found it meant 'a gift from God/of the Gods'.

A little later I was having a cup of tea when a nurse asked if some first-time mothers could come into see the twins. They trooped in and were staring in awe at me, saying, 'Oh my God! I can't believe you just had twins.' I smiled and thought to myself, *if you only knew*. This was so far removed from when I would have been dropped off outside the hospital and left completely alone to go through everything. As soon as he could, Karl got on the phone to ring everyone he knew. I received visitors and lots of presents and really enjoyed the experience. Also I knew that these were my last children. There would be no more pregnancies for me. I was determined to be the mother I had always wanted to be and this was my last chance to do it. To that end I spent a lot of time telling these babies that they were fabulous and gorgeous, determined to instil confidence in them, something I felt I had failed to do with the others.

When she was a toddler I used to put Amber on my knee and ask her 'Who is beautiful? Who is fabulous? Who is amazing? Who is gorgeous?' She would beam at me and say, 'Me, Mammy! Me!' A few years ago she gave me a Mother's Day card in which she had written all those questions out, but, this time, they were for me to answer, 'Me, Amber! Me!' I treasure it.

The rest of the kids were delighted with the babies while for me and Karl, it was hard, hard work. Nathaniel had a sleep disorder so I had to move him away from Amber because he kept waking her up. I never stopped being afraid that I would slip down into a dark hole; it became my biggest fear. My therapist worked on me a lot and made me aware of the signs that would alert me to the fact that I was slipping down again. They included shutting myself down and refusing to talk to anyone. Also, I would start to experience intense feelings of isolation before being overwhelmed by a desire to run away or kill myself. I remember when Karl and the kids were really happy, I would watch them as if I was watching a film and waiting for the evil twist. When people asked us how many children we had Karl would cheerfully blurt out seven while I only ever admitted to having 'a few'. In my mind I was carrying a stigma and I could still hear McDarby's voice putting me down.

I rang Mother after the wedding to ask her why she never showed up. She said she was sorry, a word I had heard once too often over the years. She added that she had every intention of going, but then had ended up getting drunk. Her sister had called in for her, but the house was all locked up and there was no answer to her knocking. My mother was such a disappointment to me yet I never gave up wanting her love. Over the years I bought plenty of Mother's Day cards, but rarely sent any of them since she didn't deserve them. Nevertheless, I never stopped buying them.

The three times I tried to include her in my family were pretty much regretful. Before we had a car, she got the train to Dublin and Karl took Ashley in a taxi in to collect her from the station. As soon as she climbed into the back seat she started asking Ashley if

Karl had ever touched her. Karl warned her to stop, but she ignored him and said to Ashley, 'You can tell me, you can tell me.' Naturally enough the taxi-man shot Karl a quizzical look, but Karl just told him that Mother was drunk and to keep driving. By this stage Karl knew that Mother was not the pleasant, amiable woman that he met that first time in Ardee. He knew that she was an alcoholic. It took thirty minutes to reach the house where I was nervously waiting. When Mother got out of the taxi she started roaring at me. Karl stormed past me and Ashley was in a state. Terrified of the neighbours seeing any of this, I ran to get Mother indoors as fast as I could. Meanwhile Karl was inside, going through her bag and emptying all the bottles of alcohol into the sink. I rang a friend to come and help us out. Mother had only just arrived and I already had no idea how I was going to cope with her. She was calling me names and displaying the usual rage towards me. Karl had never seen her like this before and was shocked. Turning to me, he said, 'Now I understand how he was able to do what he did to you and why you said nothing to her.'

When my friend arrived we tried to keep Mother from leaving the house, but she got out somehow and we had to follow her up the road. She spotted a phone box and rang Ardee to tell my stepfather that she was in his other house and bombarded him with the worst type of language. My friend, whose own mother had a drinking problem, had never seen or heard anything like this. In the end Mother stayed the night with us. I found some vodka that Karl had missed and gave it to her since my children had to be able to sleep. Next day we were so desperate we paid for a taxi to take her all the way back to Ardee. As usual, she had no memory of what she had said or done and was feeling very sorry for herself because I was sending her home.

Later on, when Karl bought a mobile home by the sea in Curracloe, Wexford, we decided to take the kids down there for the first weekend. I was feeling stronger in myself and thought it would be a good opportunity to include Mother. We drove to Ardee to pick her up and I knew she had some drink taken. In the car she put the vodka bottle to her mouth and I braced myself. By the time we reached Dublin again I was worried, but we picked up the kids from school, re-introducing the older ones to their grandmother. The girls got in the back with her and she started on them immediately, asking them if Karl ever hurt or touched them. Naturally they didn't know what she was talking about. I told her to stop and she exploded, screaming at the kids that they were her husband's bastards. Karl had to threaten to drop her off at the next Garda station before she quietened down.

There was one part of me that felt sorry for this sad, embittered woman who was permanently tied to a bottle of vodka. The other part of me, however, hated the drunken abusive woman. When sober she was pathetic and sorrowful. Either drunk or sober, she had no courage and did not protect me in any way.

As the children got older they started to ask questions about Nana and I explained to them about her drinking habits. There was no point in sheltering them; they had seen her in action. They also asked me about Uncle Rikki. McDarby had damaged my brother emotionally and mentally and, as a result, Rikki had his own problems. We didn't see each other that much, but I remember him visiting me one day and asking me, as he gazed out the window into the back garden, 'Is that the end of your universe, Mary?'

CHAPTER FOURTEEN

I never stopped thinking about my lack of extended family. Karl pretty much handled all the communions and confirmations. He always seemed to know what to do, while I wanted to look like I did, but in reality I didn't have a clue. All the other kids had lots of relatives to visit on their special days and lots of extra presents and cards on their birthdays and for Christmas. Mother never bought any of my kids so much as a card and there was no one else around that might have done it in her stead. Perhaps the children never realised what they were missing, but I constantly compared their lives to those of their friends. However Karl and I certainly made sure they had presents from us. I knew only too well what it was like to go without receiving anything. I was still plagued by feelings of inadequacy that I wasn't good enough as a parent. For instance, Karl attended the parent/teacher meetings alone because I didn't feel up to the challenge they presented.

The house felt smaller and smaller as the children grew. They were also filling the house with their friends, which was difficult for me as I felt my space being further invaded.

With my own friends I worked on opening myself up more. I needed to talk about relationships away from Karl. I had revealed a little of what I had been through, to shocked reactions, but it was only ever the tip of the iceberg. It wasn't that I did not trust my close friends, it was more that my story was so complicated and layered that I never felt I could articulate it properly. I did not have the words. However, the flip side of this was that I was turning into a good listener for other people who wanted to talk about their worries and issues. People sought me out to confide in me, knowing that their secrets were safe with me.

Like any married couple, Karl and I had our ups and downs. I blamed myself for most of our troubles. I can be extremely stubborn, or maybe sceptical is a better word. It was, I suppose, a natural result of the abuse. Back then I had yet to work out what I wanted to do in life and I was tiring of the limits I had placed on myself. I spent entire days consumed by self-doubt. My therapist encouraged me to open up to Karl about intimacy and suggested that we take a bath together. It was along the lines of what Karl had been asking me to try, to spend some time together, naked, either watching a film or just talking to one another. This was after I had given birth to Dillon and the twins. I tried the bath idea, though I put on my favourite nightdress and kept it on in the bath. One step at a time!

Karl encouraged me to make the house a home. I would protest that it wasn't ours and what was the point in spending money on good furniture, but he would have none of this. 'We might as well pretend it is ours and have it the way we want it.' Accordingly, he dragged me around furniture shops and picked out the best sofas and dinner tables that could accommodate the lot of us. Once the brand new – and expensive – sofa was put in place in the tiny living room, Karl would invite the kids to bounce all over it, claiming that it helped them to come out of themselves. Quite a few springs were broken this way, but I had to admit that the kids had a ball doing it.

I constantly worried about the kids when they were out of the house, even if they were just playing down the road. The fear that someone would hurt them was constant. I watched them closely as a way of trying to reassure myself that they were okay. To be sure that they were really okay, I worked on my skills of observation, noting every expression and the tone of their voices. It was the only thing I felt I could do.

For years I had a recurring nightmare. I was in

a derelict house. The doors were hanging off, the windows were smashed and the floor was all torn up. I always seemed to plunge into the dream as I was desperately trying to find a good hiding place within the house. The monster never changed: he was a giant with one huge eye in the middle of his gigantic forehead and he carried a club in his hand. And the only reason he was in the house was to find me. Most nights I would just lie beneath a few planks of wood, shaking with fear, as I listened to his footsteps all around me. Near the house was a lake and this was where I would run to, to make my escape. I would break into a run and, there he would be, right behind me, running fast and full of rage. Just as he caught me I would wake up. I always woke up when I was running.

The shadows were very much around me in Monksfield. I was never afraid of them, but they became a problem when the children began to wake up in the middle of the night and tell us there was something in their room. I have always believed I could sense spirits around me, that is, the spirits of people who have passed on. It never scared me and, in fact, it is something I share with Karl. We have had a number of experiences over the years. For instance, one day Karl and I were upstairs, in Monksfield, when a large shadow appeared on the wall in front of us. We both saw it. I ran and got holy water and threw it over it, but the water splashed back on the both of us instead … which was unexpected, to say the least. So I went down to the front door, opened it and told it to get out and leave us alone. Spirits and ghosts could not scare me when I found the living so much more terrifying.

My stepfather continued to ring the house, telling Karl and me to get out of his house. If I answered the phone he would ask me what I was doing with Karl. He was stuck in his sickness and his calls were like a broken record. The only difference that crept into his conversations was his threats to kill himself. I would put down the phone feeling miserable and guilty. I was still trying to get maintenance out of him, but he was refusing to give me a penny after I had had the audacity to actually marry Karl. This proved to me that it was all about owning me. He showed no concern over his children or the consequences of withholding money from them. It was merely his way of trying to regain control over me. The worse thing was that I believed he could see right through me. He understood when I was having a particularly bad or vulnerable day and I think he even understood my shame. I was the product of his abuse and so, in a way, I carried the shame for him: layers and layers of shame that required years of therapy and hard, hard work.

I suppose it was inevitable that I grew frightened for my girls as I watched them grow and their bodies develop. How was I going to cope with all these fears? I knew what men were capable of. What could I say to them, or not say to them? It became impossible for me not to constantly compare my teenage years to theirs. It was like I had one foot stuck in my past, which was doing its best to flood and contaminate my present. How I yearned to have a mother that I could discuss my worries with.

But I had Karl. He was branching out as a successful educator and lecturer. And he used his expertise to bring me out of myself. Karl was able to read people and he would also sense things, things that had yet to happen. One time when I was having a particularly dark day, he got a pen and paper and started to draw circles representing the things and people in my life. The bigger the circle, the bigger the space it had in my life. Not too surprisingly, the circle representing my stepfather was huge. Next in size were Karl's and each of the kids'. After that it was my meetings followed by one or two close friends. Then he began to tell me my future as if he was telling me a story. Where would I be in five years, ten years and twenty years? As he spoke, McDarby's circle grew smaller and smaller while Karl's and the kids' increased in size. He began to add lots of other circles, telling me that these represented the different people I would help and the many things I would go on to do. He told me I would heal lots of people and here he drew a circle representing my gifts, assuring me that there was a new and exciting life ahead for me. I just sat there crying, because I did not believe it. I did not feel special nor did I feel gifted in any way, shape or form, but he promised me it was true, that it was definitely going to happen. 'All I'm asking you to do right now is believe in yourself. Because I do.' I pretended to believe for his sake, but I didn't, not yet anyway.

Apart from telling me that I was too ugly for anyone to ever like me, McDarby also told me, over and over again, that I was stupid. This was possibly one of the reasons I felt drawn to further education. My Leaving Certificate had been a disaster because I was pregnant and traumatised, yet I knew I had been clever before this and that I had a keen brain. I did have an interest in history and science, but had never got a chance to explore this. McDarby had stripped me of having choices regarding my education. The irony is that money was not a problem; I could have gone to college if I wasn't being eroded as an independent person. Furthermore I was pretty sure that my father, as a self-taught businessman, would have wanted and encouraged me to go to college because he wanted the best for his kids. Deciding that I would return to education was a healing in itself. I was taking a massive step to confront my stepfather and his brainwashing in that I had to believe I was good enough in order to be able to apply. The rest of my life was not going to be about me surviving my past – I wanted to live too and be a productive member of society.

I started off small, with a short course in arts and crafts. I had seen a poster for it and decided to do it. It was just a short course, once a week for eight weeks, but it was a real accomplishment for me. The first week I was so nervous. It was quite a big class and most of them were older than me, but I thoroughly enjoyed it. I made a centrepiece for the Christmas table, which I still have to this day. It's a bit worn now, but Karl insists on using it every year. The course was an important step forward, allowing me to start believing that there was something more to me than being a mother and a victim. I can do this! Also, it brought out my creative side. I have come to believe that creativity, sensuality, sexuality and spirituality are a vital part of each and every person and it is of the utmost importance to nurture all of them. They are all different forms of expression and, I suppose, require a language that I was only beginning to learn because of my stunted background. This little course in arts and crafts awakened something within me on a spiritual level. Up to then I did not actually believe in 'a God, but I began to feel a loving presence beside me and I could see colours around the various people I was coming into contact with. I felt it was an angelic presence, my guardian angel and so forth. They did not intrude on me, but I felt their gentle care and love. It was not a big deal, but it certainly was a soothing accompaniment to my day. The others in the class were so friendly and I must have appeared normal, since they treated me as if I was a proper member of the group. It provided the most wonderful contrast to my world of McDarby and abuse.

From arts and crafts I went on to do a course in social studies in the local community centre. Karl was so encouraging and told me that I could do whatever I wanted. It was, I think, a year-long course and covered subjects like child psychology and development. Again, I thoroughly enjoyed it and found I had a good brain for reading and studying. I still expected to appear abnormal in comparison to the other students and I worried that they could see I was different in some way. However, Karl kept at me, telling me that it did not matter whether I passed or failed the exam because the most important thing was my actually doing it and finding out if I liked it or not.

Now I was on a roll. Before the social studies course ended I found out about a short course in criminal law that was being run in University College Dublin (UCD). Because of my experience I was eager to learn more about law and I put my name down for it. This was a step up from the local community centre because I had to get a bus to somewhere I had never been before. It was a bit of an ordeal, but I did it and it really was thrilling to find out that I was not stupid. McDarby was wrong about that. I understood what my lecturers were saying and was extremely grateful for that fact. However the course was not what I was particularly interested in. One day, in UCD, I found out about a two-year course in Neuro-linguistic Programming (NLP) counselling and hypnotherapy that was taking place in Milltown. NLP is an approach to self-development and psychotherapy that believes in a connection between the brain, language and behaviour patterns that have been learned through experience. I signed up to do it and found it fascinating, but could only afford to do it for eighteen months due to the price of it. One lasting benefit of this course, however, was that I met Judith who remains one of my closest friends today and is actually Amber's godmother. We clicked immediately, both sensing that the other was different … in a good way. I dressed older than my years, mostly in black and purple, while she wore all the colours of the rainbow. We laughed a lot. I called her a hippie and she called me a white witch. Today she is an incredible youth worker. So, this was the type of person I was starting to attract into my life.

It would not be the only time that I would be called a white witch. A 'white witch' is – if you like, a 'good' witch – that is, someone who believes in the power of healing others and is only interested in using spells and/or plants to do good. For instance, if my grandmother had lived in the seventeenth century she might have been accused of being a witch, such was her knowledge regarding plants and healing.

At a meeting of Alcoholics Anonymous (AA) I met Clint, who became a huge influence and inspiration for me and is the only other man on this planet who knows as much about me as Karl does. A country man,

Clint does not believe in talking just for the sake of filling pauses, but when he does speak it is always full of honesty and sense. Over the years he has been a constant teacher to me, explaining to me the importance of nature in our world, as my grandmother used to do, the role that trees play, and it was he who taught me about 'Om', the divine first word of God that can be used as a mantra to meditate with. He obviously recognised something different in me too and told me that he felt I was a white witch. Even today when I get sad, mad or scared, I'll ring him for his advice which can be as blunt and bald as, 'Just turn left, Mary!'

It took me a while to understand that these special, gifted people were coming into my life to show me that I was also gifted and that I was someone special too.

I found things to do on the dark days when I felt scared and sad. I started to collect *Bunty* annuals, from the popular comics that were published from 1958 to 2001. I actually have one from 1958. Friends would buy them for me if they spotted them in second-hand book shops. I also collected the Disney films on video and then on DVD. They never failed to comfort me on the bad days. *Cinderella* and *Beauty and the Beast* are probably my favourites as these particular stories resonated with me. The beast was just someone who was afraid, like me, to show his true self to the world.

Meanwhile my case was still ongoing and I hoped to get justice at some stage. I had accepted the fact that McDarby would not be locked up, but I hoped that the other names would be compelled to admit that they had not done their best by me. One natural consequence of all this education was that I was learning how I had been wronged by the system and not just by one person, but right across the board. I put my trust in my new solicitor, yet I could not help wishing that he would be a bit more like my previous one. Nevertheless, I recognised that people are different and have their own strengths so I did not doubt that he was doing his best for me, in his own way. During our phone calls we had talked about looking for some sort of financial settlement from McDarby and having him comply with a maintenance order. My solicitor guided me through this. Winning a maintenance order would, we felt, strengthen the civil action case against everyone else.

Some years had passed since I first made that statement in 1993. The twins were now six years old. I was busy studying. We had a mobile home in Wexford where we spent the summers, and life, on the surface, was more normal than it ever had been. I was still seeing my therapist and attending workshops. The people on the list had been served with summons and affidavits and so forth. The kids were relatively happy and I was working on being a better partner to Karl. I focussed on being more open and we did do a lot of talking where I would examine the past as much as I could, in order to free me up a little more for the present. Of course I was still a busy mother, spending hours making dinners, ironing, laundry, washing, cleaning, checking homework and making sure that everyone was okay.

The girls were still wards of court under the health board who wanted to revoke the order so that they could wash their hands of them. However, Carmel, the social worker, told me not to revoke it since I still needed help. Because I had no family support, the friends that were around Karl and I became like family to us. Karl was still angry about my past and the DPP while I didn't want to dwell on it. This created tension. He had taken on my four children and that was tough on a budding relationship. Sometimes it felt that we had skipped a chunk of time that would have involved just the two of us being with one another. My situation had required us to jump in with two feet without taking the time to think or negotiate each other's feelings. I depended on him so much. As the kids got older there were inevitable issues. Of course I had to blind myself to McDarby's likeness in the older ones and that took time. Then there was the fact that they called Karl 'Karl' while the others called him 'Dad' and this was something that had to be discussed.

Following some agonising I let Karl tell the children the truth about me and my stepfather, their father. I could not have done it myself, but we both wanted them to know the truth. It had to come out because there was no father's name on the birth certificates for Rory, Iseult, Ashley and Megan. Now, they knew that McDarby was their father, but didn't know that he was my stepfather and certainly had no idea that they were the product of violent rapes that had begun when I was a little girl. Also they had seen the emotional states I had fallen into over the years and deserved a proper explanation. I wanted them to understand that I had not lied to them in any way, I had simply felt they had to reach a certain age and understanding to hear the story. Karl also told them about Andrew, but they had no clear memories about him. Only Ashley remembered him with any clarity.

In any case they had a chance to make sense of why

they had ended up in care and why, unlike their friends, they did not receive visits from doting grandparents or aunts and uncles. They knew that Uncle Rikki was always sad and now the four older ones had to digest the fact that Uncle James is actually their half-brother. It was out in the open, the effect my life of abuse had had on theirs. I found it a little terrifying although I suppose it was also a release of some kind. Both Karl and I had long decided that our home would be an honest one, where nobody would be afraid to speak the truth. There was no support group I could send the children to. The likes of Rainbows did not cover topics like how to cope with a mother who has been traumatised for years by her stepfather who is also her children's father.

I wanted to beg their forgiveness, if only for the fact that we were struggling to give them all the stuff I yearned to. Whatever else you could say about my tragic past, I had come from money and I hated not being able to buy my children whatever I wanted to. There was also the matter that I did not want to look like a victim or someone in need. I wanted to look like I had had a good and normal life, but it was hard to do so on our budget. I had a picture in my head of how I wanted to look, but it was financially unrealistic and I struggled with that too.

At some point I started going to Adult Children of Alcoholics (ACOA) meetings. I went quite regularly on top of my therapy and I did get a lot out of them. The meetings were on a Friday night and they became an important part of my week. I learned how alcoholism affects people and their families. My mother's addiction left me open to my stepfather's sadism and violence. I discussed her alcoholism in the meetings and only said that she did not protect me, but I never said from whom. An important part of the meetings was my getting a chance to listen to other people's experiences. It was a safe atmosphere in which to open up, in front of the group, about how Mother's drinking had affected me.

I was full of rage for her because she had failed to protect me in every way possible and I was holding on to that anger with both hands. At the same time I could not find that same anger for my stepfather because I still needed him financially. He had implemented a regime that had begun when I was ten years old and it was ingrained. I blamed myself for what he did to me and I was still ashamed about the kids. Even at these meetings I could not bring myself to admit to how many children I had. To be honest it is still something that can challenge me today. When I do manage to say the number 'seven' I – sometimes – have to grin and bear a shocked expression or a nervous laugh, or a silly comment along the lines of 'Oh my God! There must have been no television in your house!'

My inability to properly open up did frustrate me. Also the fact that I was still consumed by darkness and doubt made me afraid about the rest of my life. Would I ever change or was I cursed forever? Eventually I went to a priest and told him that I was scared I might be possessed. He advised me to go home, light three candles and say some prayers. And then he gave me the most wonderful message, 'Don't worry, Mary. Your spirit is coming home.'

CHAPTER FIFTEEN

There is a Native American story involving a grandfather explaining to his grandson about the fact that we all have two sides to us. He tells him, 'Two wolves exist within me. One is big and strong, but he is always angry and fights over every little thing, hurting those around him with his temper. The second wolf is small and quiet and believes in living in a state of peace. He wishes only to bring love and kindness to all. However, the bad wolf constantly fights the good wolf and only one of them can survive.' The child listens to this and then asks, 'Which one will survive, grandfather?' The old man smiles and tells him, 'The one you feed.'

I had begun the work of feeding the good wolf, and it was truly a work-in-progress.

In 2001 I nervously walked through the archway of Trinity College in order to start my diploma on addiction studies. I was both excited and terrified. Karl kept telling me that I would be great and not to waste energy feeling that I wasn't good enough. He gave me all the directions I needed, along with a friend of mine who tutored in the college. I prayed my shyness would not hold me back and asked God and the angels to give me the courage I needed. Nevertheless, I could not deny that I felt ready for this.

It was my friend Steven who suggested that I apply to come here. He had been telling for ages that I clearly had a gift for healing people by helping to unblock their emotions, even when they themselves did not recognise what they were feeling. It was true. People sought me out to tell me their worries and problems and somehow I helped them. Call it intuition or instinct, but I could sense why they were in pain; I knew it before they did. Months beforehand, Karl had been working on a drugs project out in Monkstown and they needed a counsellor to do one-on-one work with the clients there. Thanks to him I got the job and loved it. I would sit with these people who believed that they had nothing left to live for and I could *see* them. Before they started talking I could see their pain and the journeys they were on. They opened up to me – the addicts and their families – and I learned so much from them. Some people have had to deal with the most extraordinary struggles on a daily basis. I could see what they had braved in order to sit in the room with me. It was a privilege and absolutely cemented the notion I had of helping people. I knew now exactly what I wanted to do and Trinity College was going to help get me there.

Steven and Karl believed that helping people was my true path in life. It certainly seemed like I was being spiritually guided and that every step I had taken previously had led me to walking across these well-worn cobbles in the campus courtyard, feeling full of hope and butterflies.

The biggest obstacle I had to climb, that first morning, was the usual feeling that I might stick out and that people might guess I had a dark and secret past. I also had to keep reminding myself that I wasn't stupid, that I had already proved this much to myself. It was scary, all those people milling around who seemed to know one another. The noise was tremendous. Because it was the first day it was mostly about being introduced to our timetable, our lecturers and to each other. We also had to be shown the different locations for the different lectures. For a couple of subjects we had to leave Trinity and cross the busy road outside to other buildings.

The class was a good mixture of age and experience. At one point we had to stand up and give our name and the reason we were there. We also had to talk about ourselves to the person next to us and have them talk about themselves, all little ice-breakers that I would have been familiar with from my sessions and workshops at the Rape Crisis Centre. It fascinated me how some people had no fear when it came to asking questions. We were barely in the door, barely handed the timetable and the questions began. I admired their courage, but also thought some of the questions were a little premature. Lunchtime was another ordeal. I mostly kept to myself, but enjoyed watching how other people behaved. Again there were the confident ones who seemed to make connections immediately and spent the lunchhour yapping away as if they had been doing this for years. I took my time, not because I didn't want to be liked, but because I had no idea how to push myself forward.

I remember going into the library during my first week, and revelling in the smell of books and history. This was where the famous *Book of Kells* was held. How many people had browsed these shelves before me? I was a frequent visitor to the library thereafter. Everything delighted me about the college: the architecture, the atmosphere and the shiny parquet floor. Groups of tourists would come up behind me, obliging me to move aside to allow them room to pass before returning to where I had been standing so that I could continue to enjoy the spectacle. I hoped the tourists could see that I – Mary Manning – was a student here. It was surreal that I was standing in Trinity College, my bag full of copies and pens. I fell in love with the place. It became a little piece of heaven for me.

Gradually I began to make friends. My lecturers would probably say I was quiet in class. I watched others ask questions or provide answers while I preferred to take it all in. I spoke when I was called upon, but I don't think I ever volunteered information. There was always so much happening around the campus plus there were plenty of mature students like me, so I didn't feel that I stuck out from everyone else. After a while I genuinely felt I belonged.

The reason I chose that particular course was that I had become interested in addiction. I wanted to find out as much as I could about addictions, and the effects they had on people's lives. Of course this interest must have sprung from my experience with my mother. I was curious as to how somebody could be so affected by drink or drugs. I was interested in people and what made them tick. And I could not forget my own journey in America when I used both alcohol and drugs to block out my own pain. That provided me with first-hand experience of how things could, step by step, spiral out of control. My least favourite part of the course was the role playing which forced me to speak in front of the class. Otherwise I loved it and found that my listening and observational skills were finely tuned.

It was hard work. The course was full-time, Monday to Friday, and I still had a house to keep and children to be there for. Actually it was utterly exhausting, but I suppose when you are pursuing something you are passionate about, you find the energy and the time to fit it in with all the other day-to-day stuff that still had to be done.

At the end of the year I had to give a presentation in front of the class. The night before I practised in front of Karl and kids and panicked slightly when I kept laughing and had to start over again. The kids had enough after three hours of this, but Karl hung in there and I eventually made it to the end. Of course I was in bits again the next morning. Nevertheless, I did it. I wasn't sure if anything would come out of my mouth when I was called to stand up, but fortunately once I got the first sentence out perfectly I was fine after that.

Education certainly freed some part of me, but the rest of me was still enmeshed in darkness and still feeling trapped. My life had not been resolved. McDarby was still out there doing whatever he wanted without having faced any consequences for what he had put me through. It was something that stuck in my gut; the fact that he had got away with everything. That was my thinking; you could do whatever you wanted in this country once you didn't get caught doing it.

In 2002 my solicitor rang me to tell me that McDarby had finally agreed to give me a settlement for damages done. He believed that I should accept it as it would further strengthen my case in court. I would receive €140,000 and a maintenance order for so much per month. Freedom beckoned. The money meant that Karl and I could go looking for our own house. I was desperate for a bigger house and one that was not in Dublin. It did take quite a while before the paperwork went through and the money went into my account. Regarding houses, all I knew was that I wanted a nice one, one I could be proud of, and it couldn't be in a housing estate, but it had to be within commutable distance of Dublin. Karl was able to get a mortgage on top of the settlement, allowing us to make our first real fresh start as a couple.

The civil action case was still pending and there

was a part of me that worried I was selling out too soon. However, I could not argue with the fact that my own solicitor felt it would actually strengthen the civil action case in court.

I met my old social worker, Carmel M, at my graduation ceremony because a relative of hers was also graduating. We hadn't seen one another in a couple of years and ended up drinking tea afterwards in Trinity. 'Oh, my God!', she gasped, 'When I heard the name Mary Manning, I immediately wondered if it could possibly be you?' She was so genuinely proud of me, which really touched me.

Karl, who knew my taste in jewellery, presented me with a dainty antique rose-gold necklace, showing me that this was an exciting day to be celebrated. I was only allowed to bring two people with me, but Karl managed to sneak Iseult and Ashley in with himself. The girls were so excited to be there while I experienced a mix of emotions. I don't think I ever actually said to myself, *Wow – you've done it, you've reecived a diploma from Trinity College*! Of course I put a smile on my face and the ceremony was lovely, but still I felt sadness. As I stood there, I remembered the low points and how hard I had struggled at times, how I had needed Karl's help with essays or with doing presentations. I'm not sure if I was feeling sceptical about the day, it was more that I kept a lid on any potentially happy emotions by reminding myself that this was just about getting a piece of paper for doing a diploma course in addictions studies and that was all. I looked around at my classmates' obvious delight and it seemed to me that they felt this was a huge, massive thing in their lives, but I could not, or would not, allow myself to share that perception.

I refused to wear the cap and gown. It just wasn't me and I dreaded going up to get my diploma. I wasn't fully in the zone of celebration, yet there was a part of me that was excited. When my name was called I managed to get to my feet and walk up those steps and to collect my piece of paper with gratitude. It was a huge achievement, but I don't think I gave myself enough credit at the time. In fact, I know I didn't.

During the academic year I discovered that I needed to find myself a three-month placement for my work experience. A variety of locations were on offer that included America, Australia and Britain, but, in the end, I went for the Rutland Centre in Dublin, the largest rehabilitation centre in Ireland. I sent in my application and was called for an interview and succeeded in winning a placement there. This meant that I would be working one-on-one with individuals and doing group work as well as giving lectures. I reckoned it would give me the confidence boost that I needed.

I found the house I was searching for – a bungalow sitting on an acre of land. The first thing that attracted me was the large bathroom that was tiled in black and white and had a heart-shaped bath that sparkled. There were wooden floors throughout, spacious rooms and the main bedroom had its own *en suite*. Karl had fallen for a bigger house that had six bedrooms, more than enough room for everybody, but it was in the middle of nowhere and further from Dublin than I wanted to be. We did put in an offer for that house and I was relieved when it fell through. Neither of us had any idea how much work was involved in buying a house and then moving into it. Also, we were not prepared for the fact that we had to pay my solicitor quite a few grand so we had less money than we thought, plus we needed to buy new furniture. Just before we moved I had to get my therapist, who was a priest, to baptise the twins so that they could make their Holy Communion. Karl was working so hard and there were a bewildering amount of certificates required. The paperwork seemed endless.

Then sixteen-year-old Iseult, who was in secondary school, dropped the bombshell that she could not come with us because she was in fifth year – in other words she was less than a year away from doing her Leaving Certificate examination. In any case I knew she was far from happy about moving because she didn't want to leave her friends. It was a problem and a half. In the end we made the big decision to leave her in the house and allow her to finish her schooling without any interruption. It was not an easy decision, but it seemed like the only solution. The house in Monksfield belonged to her father who was not allowed near it and she felt safe there. One of her teachers needed somebody to take his dog and inevitably Iseult volunteered to keep him. She was always mad about animals and, as a child, filled her pockets with 'rescued' caterpillar families. Also my brother James moved in to be there with her. It was not an ideal situation, but she visited us every weekend.

Apart from leaving Iseult behind I was extremely upbeat about the move. As far as I was concerned this new house represented our first real home as a couple and a family. It had not been touched by McDarby in any way and, therefore, there were no negative associations. This was the fresh new start that Karl and I had craved. We did up the interior in bright colours while Karl set to work in the garden, planting apples trees for each of the kids. He sectioned off an orchard for them and put in a berry garden, planting lots of trees and shrubs. Eventually we built a wall around it. Today the garden resembles my grandmother's herb-jungle in Ardee, with lots of nooks and crannies and is a real treasure trove in the summer. We also built a log cabin to give the older kids somewhere private to go and it was no ordinary cabin. It had its own bathroom, bedroom and a small kitchen-cum-living room.

It took the kids a while to adjust to living in a small country village. I was still extremely protective of them, which motivated me to want a wall of huge slabs built around the garden. Clint, my friend, was visiting me and laughed, 'You don't put up walls in the countryside!' I replied, 'You might not, but I do!' So this was still the remnants of the abuse following me to our new home. I was still in therapy and doing lots of work on coming more into society and finding a way to 'really' live and be fully engaged with my circum-stances. No longer could I be a robot that performed duties without interest or passion. More was required of me now from this new life I was putting together for myself. I still had my days when I tumbled into inadequacy, only believing that if I could change my past everything would be absolutely great.

Perhaps it was around this time that I began to develop a fondness for flamboyant shoes and nice clothes. I did not choose my past nor how it had affected me, but I could damn well choose how I presented myself to the world. I was determined to keep my scars on the inside and never allow myself to look like a victim or someone who had had a tough life. Lying in bed at night I would battle these fears about not being good enough for my job, friends and family. When I got up in the morning I would hide them away behind carefully applied make-up, nails, false tan, glamorous high-heeled shoes and designer clothes. When I stepped out my front door, nobody would have been able to guess what had happened to me.

Another milestone had been getting a car, albeit a small one. I got it before the move and now was able to drive myself to the centre and back again. How I relished the independence and the freedom that came with this. I passed the test on my first attempt. When I took to the road I could not help thinking that this was another way of proving to my stepfather that I wasn't stupid.

Thinking about that first car reminds me of a journey I took one day, I don't remember where I was going, but I do remember glancing in my rearview mirror and realising, with a start, that I was not expecting to see my stepfather's face behind me. It also struck me that he wasn't in my thoughts all day, every day, like he used to be. The bond was definitely loosening what with my newfound confidence and lease of life. Learning to drive and sitting at the wheel of my own car was an important step for me. On a metaphorical level I suppose you could say that at long last I was in the driving seat after a lifetime of being driven around by him, with no control over my destination.

I still tried to find a connection with my mother. I wanted her to see my new house, but every time I rang her she would be drunk and abusive to me. It didn't stop me from trying again a few weeks later. In fact I was probably a little apathetic to her behaviour, only thinking to myself, 'Ah, well. Fair enough!' as I hung up on her. At this stage, what was the point in getting upset. Learning to live involved my not entertaining or having big responses to things. This also meant that I could not have shown real joy in anything either. It was all about keeping myself on an even keel.

Because it had taken so long to get the settlement

and then the actual physical money into my account, I began to think that the civil action case was going to take ages more since it involved so many groups including the DPP, the Attorney General, the Health Board and a few doctors. Would it ever be resolved? The older I got the more I yearned for justice. I wanted my voice to be heard for once in my life. Karl never stopped doubting that I would be looked after and it would all work out to my advantage. He has lost his raw rage over the DPP and was probably, like me, a little worn out after all the years of anger.

Meanwhile I was nervous about the placement and desperately wanted to only do my very best. I still felt I was hiding my past and that it would come out that I was a fraud, but I needn't have worried. My supervisor, an older lady called Ann M, saw something in me despite the fact that I lacked confidence in myself. I used to study the other counsellors and marvel at their sense of self. All the staff made me feel welcome and they genuinely seemed to like me too. I made some good friends that are still in my life today. Ann, in particular, took me under her wing. It was the first time that I felt nurtured and mothered since Grandma and Ann remains my dear friend to this day. She supervised my group sessions and was pleased with what she saw. I broke down in front of her when she told me, 'There's something very special about you, Mary Manning!' She would tell me over and over again that I had a gift for dealing with people. Recognising that I lacked confidence, she did her best to make me feel stronger in myself. If there were work parties, she would inform me we were going together and I was to hold my head up high and enjoy myself.

Ann became a mentor to me. I tried my best to imitate her. I loved how she dressed and how she did her hair. She didn't judge me and I ended up telling her pretty much everything. She was appalled at what I had had to deal with. Of course, my experiences helped me to recognise when other people were trying to deal with the consequences of trauma. I could spot trauma right away from the slightest flicker of an eyelash or the tiniest movement of a finger. When a person is in pain their interior world makes it way to the exterior, but you have to know what you are looking for in order to see it. And I did because I had been there.

My placement lasted three months, but then they offered me a job to do locum. This meant that I would cover sick leave and holidays and since there were a few staff off sick longterm there was quite a workload to be dealt with. In any case, I had to admit to myself

– however grudgingly – that I must have been doing something right.

CHAPTER SIXTEEN

About a year after I got my diploma from Trinity I decided to do a three-year course in psychotherapy at the Tivoli Institute in Dun Laoghaire. I was looking for the best course available and this was it. It was accredited and widely recognised and the name of the college repeatedly popped up when I researched courses on psychotherapy. Despite the fact that the Rutland Centre gave me a job I still felt inadequate when I compared myself to the other counsellors. This resulted in my decision to do more study.

If I thought the previous year was tough, it was nothing compared to the following three years when I kept up my full-time job in the Rutland alongside my course. The course involved going to lectures two weekends a month and attending summer schools. Sundays were all-day group sessions. There were pleasant discoveries awaiting me as I embarked on this course. Frequently I attended a lecture to learn that I was already doing whatever they were talking about ,only I had assumed it was natural and had placed no particular importance on it. Now, thanks to the Tivoli,

I had nice names for what I was already practising with my clients in the Rutland. It was a welcome confirmation for me that I was doing something good and right.

Subjects included human development, child and adult psychology, abnormal and deviant psychology. I attended lots and lots of lectures and wrote lots and lots of essays. There were continuous assessments, placements and role play. I made some good friends at the Tivoli, but not as many as I had expected. Essays were researched and written alongside hours and hours of study, while also carrying out the regular stuff with the kids and never-ending housework, though Karl did more than his fair share in this regard, what with all the cooking, minding, tidying and delegating as well, of course, as his own job. However, I truly loved what I was doing. I got so much from helping people and I started to believe that my life was worthwhile. As I watched my clients facing into hard situations and the harsh realities that made up their lives, I would feel the energy building inside me and my desire to help them face up to things. Now, it wasn't perfect. Every now and then I still heard McDarby's voice in my head telling me I was a nobody, and I still had my bleak days when I felt I would never be good enough to do anything of merit, but, somehow, I managed to keep going. Those two words were almost a mantra for me, 'keep going'. Although McDarby's voice haunted me when I was feeling vulnerable it had admittedly lost a lot of its power. In fact I began to feel sorry for him and his narrow-mindedness. I was able to take a step back and see how messed up he was. His power was starting to fade, but I still doubted myself on my bad days.

It was around this time that Mother was taken into hospital. She was still drinking despite the fact she was being treated for sclerosis of the liver. In fact, she became a regular visitor to hospital. Not surprisingly, the years of drinking were starting to take their toll on her body. She began to look like an alcoholic and there followed a pattern of her taking bad falls around the house. I have to admit that my patience was stretched thin, while Karl never failed to respond to the phone calls from the hospital that became more and more frequent. It got to the stage where he would take the call and go out and buy her a small suitcase along with toiletries and a choice of nighties. I begrudged spending money on her and certainly felt that she did not deserve a *choice* of nightgowns. I was so angry at her, but, at the same time, I did not actually want her to suffer. After all my studying and dealing with addicts and alcoholics, I still hoped that she could stop drinking in time to be the mother I had always yearned for.

My own health started to trouble me with heavy bleeds in between periods. I went for tests and nobody could work out the cause of this, though I absolutely believed that it was from the years of abuse. Despite all this I kept up a tremendous pace in work. Because I wanted to do well and be liked I turned into a 'Yes' person: yes, I'll do group work; yes, I'll do relapse prevention; yes, I, do the evening sessions and the day sessions. Looking back, I think I was compensating for what I felt were gaps in my Trinity year. I had befriended a tutor and she, along with Karl, had helped me with my essays, the indexing and the referencing. Because of this I did not feel I had been fully capable of doing the diploma and now wanted to make up for it. Of course this ate into my family time, as I began to stay regularly in the house in Dublin to accommodate night classes and the early morning ones. When I finally got home I was utterly exhausted.

However I did feel I had achieved what I wanted: I was now a fully-fledged productive member of society. People respected me in the Rutland as a peer and as a counsellor. My clients seemed to connect with me on more than one level, which made my job even more rewarding.

CHAPTER SEVENTEEN

Finally, my solicitor had some news about my case and wanted me to meet with our senior counsel in the Four Courts in Dublin. The meeting was set for 3pm in the law library. It took us ages to locate the library and my solicitor, but eventually Karl and I spotted him in his pinstriped suit, in deep conversation with an older man who was wearing the black gown of a barrister. When we approached them he asked could we give him a few minutes as he was talking with my senior counsel. I had been waiting years for this, so a few minutes more was neither here nor there.

We moved off to give them privacy and I studied my senior counsel from where we stood, trying to get a sense of him through his body language. This was the man whom my solicitor had chosen to fight for me in court. Actually, we should have met years earlier when the papers were first served to those names on my original solicitor's list.

My solicitor called for Karl and I to join them. To my surprise and bewilderment my senior counsel started off the conversation by explaining he was only stepping in to help a friend. This threw me, but not as much as what he said next. 'Ms Manning, I must inform you that due to the delay in bringing me onboard, you are entitled to change your solicitor, should you wish to.' I could not make sense of this. He added, 'I have only this afternoon been asked to step in and present your case. I will do what I can, but naturally I have little understanding of your story. Having briefly read your file I would recommend that you strike off some of those names that you planned to take action against because I do not have enough time to summon the expert witnesses required.'

I was stunned. What on earth was he talking about? Hadn't I provided all the reports and paperwork I had been asked to? As far as I was concerned they had everything they needed.

He said a whole lot of other stuff, but it went over my head.

My reaction was typical. *Here we go again. It was fucked up! I should have known.* I don't think I fully understood what was being said to me and I possibly switched off for the full explanation. When I got home, Iseult was angry with me because I had so little information while Karl did his best to relate what had happened. No doubt I let it go over my head because

I felt it was the same crap all over again. All these years later and I was still losing out to McDarby.

A few days later, Karl, Iseult, Megan and I were in court for the hearing. Not surprisingly I was carrying a lot of anxiety; my shoulders felt like they were supporting a heavy burden. Of course I was dreading the day ahead, having no idea what to expect. Also, I had been in two minds about Iseult and Megan accompanying us, but they had absolutely insisted and so I gave in, feeling grateful in any case for their solid support. Karl kept checking I was alright, asking me what I was thinking and so on. However I was not in the mood to divulge my thoughts and only wanted to be left alone with them. Perhaps my biggest challenge was to ignore the fact that I had lost a lot of faith in the Irish legal system.

Karl parked the car nearby and I walked behind my family who were cracking jokes amongst themselves, no doubt doing their best to distract me from myself, but I only felt a mental distance open up between the three of them and me. How could they laugh at a time like this, didn't they realise how hugely important and serious this was for me?, but then they had never walked in my shoes and, therefore, could have no idea what this day meant.

Inside, my first thought was to find the bathroom and check my pink lipstick was still in place. There was no way I was going to show any cracks in my physical appearance. Karl dashed off to find out what courtroom we were in. As I retouched my lipstick I thought about how deceptive looks can be. The vivid pinkness on my lips was part of my facial armour, my mask to hide the reality of my life from those who would look upon me today. In reality I knew that if anyone chose to gaze into my eyes they would see my truth laid bare and unprotected by make-up and good clothes. Few people, however, actually look into a person's eyes so I felt safe enough. As I walked back to my family I felt confident, competent and in full control of my emotions. I smiled to myself; I was ready.

We were much too early and would have to wait around until the afternoon, when my case was going to be heard. The courtroom was not what I had expected. It was crowded and clammy in atmosphere, looking a little like a church with its rows of wooden seats all facing the raised desks at the top of the room. The judge was plump and wore glasses and seemed rather removed from the hustle and bustle. Solicitors and barristers chatted or checked their phones while there was a continuous flow of people arriving and leaving again. Karl spotted a seat at the back and we all sat pressed tightly together on a hard, wooden bench.

I felt I had been right to fear that there would be no genuine warmth or interest shown in the people whose cases were being dealt with. I had worried that the process would feel cold and rushed, people's lives being efficiently boxed away like Christmas decorations in January. As I listened to the other cases I anxiously questioned if justice could be truly handed out when the sum total of your life to date was described in one brief paragraph.

They all looked so young and inexperienced. How were they possibly going to understand my case? Briefly, I raged inwardly that I should have gone into law so that I could present my own case. All the legal jargon was mind-boggling and intended, I felt, to make people like me feel stupid. I watched the body language and the constant urgent whispering back and forth about the case in progress. A man stood near me flicking through a thick folder filled with all our files. Was there time for all these cases to be fairly judged? Whose lives would be settled today?

Two barristers fiercely debated one another over some point or other and then I watched them walk out the door planning where they would go for lunch and complimenting one another on their performance. It was as if we were all involved in some grand game with our lives, which I suppose we were. My confidence was slowly evaporating as I wondered how some law written a hundred years ago could be applied to my experience of rape and torture by my stepfather.

Due to imperfect hearing in my left ear (which was down to an untreated ear infection; Mother and McDarby ignoring the fact I was in agony) I worried that I would not be able to fully follow the proceedings. I spotted my solicitor in the crowd and he looked far from happy. Well, that was appropriate since I was not feeling happy and neither was Karl. Megan didn't really know what was going on, but Iseult was engaged in the whole thing, determined to see justice being done for her mother.

The afternoon wore on as I waited for my number to be called. Finally, it was my turn. As I had expected, once discussion got underway about my case I found it difficult to hear everything that was said. I caught snippets about my story here and there. I heard my case coupled with others cases that the State had successfully won in the past. The time delay was mentioned as well as the allegations of unanswered letters and a supposed lack of cooperation from my side ... which was new to me. The truth was beginning to unfold while my senior counsel attempted to explain to me just how the legal rules and procedures of the Court were badly affecting my case.

I struggled to understand what was being said at the top of the room. The barrister put his two hands up to the judge, as he read from his notes, asking that I be spared from having everything aired in the open court. The judge agreed to this and read my files in silence. Next he sympathised with my plight, at which point the other barrister, a young girl, informed him that I had managed to put myself through college ... making it sound like it was a bad thing for me to have done. It seemed she wanted me punished for trying to improve myself and that really, I should be happy with my lot and stop wasting the court's time. She was oblivious to the incredulous look I gave her. Did she really imagine that it had been an easy journey: that I somehow got over a decade of the most horrific abuse and skipped my way up Westmoreland Street and into Trinity College? I wanted to tell her about the years of therapy and the years of the darkest of days when I was too depressed to attempt suicide. Wasn't she lucky that she had no idea what it was like – to be nothing, to matter to absolutely no one?

In vain, I waited for my barrister to say something. Instead of standing up and saying something, he held up both hands, to show he was finished. It was all over and had taken about four minutes out of everyone's day.

Four minutes.

My case was thrown out. Furthermore, they were going to sue me for costs because of the length of time involved and the fact that my papers or affidavits, or whatever, were not served correctly.

By the time I reached our car I had shut down. Iseult said something about my solicitor suggesting that I go to the Supreme Court, but I had no interest in pursuing the matter any further. I was done. The voice in my head wanted to tell my daughter, *Listen, that was the final straw for me. I have been to hell and back and have had more than enough now. So everyone can just go jump off a cliff because I refuse to put myself through any more of this.* Iseult fought my silence, 'Mum, are you just going to give up? Please don't give up!'

I managed to answer her, 'Do you not understand? There is no point doing any more!' I badly wanted to tell her and the others to leave me alone, but that is a tough thing to say to your child who just wants the best for you. She was frustrated as tears rolled down her cheeks, but I had no words of comfort for her. I had nothing at all.

Karl was in a silent rage. I could see the white of his knuckles as he gripped the steering wheel. Iseult was angry because she felt I was refusing to listen to sense while I just felt exhausted. I was bleeding heavily again and felt suddenly wiped out on every level, emotionally, mentally and physically. Once more McDarby had proved that he could do what he wanted to me and get off completely free. Now I had to deal with the fact that all those people, social workers and doctors, who had done so little for me, were going to get off scot-free too. Why had I even bothered? I had hoped that winning the civil action case would provide me with the closure I needed. I had also hoped to clear my name. I never stopped feeling that I had been branded as being the one at fault. How naïve had I been? Now the Irish State had come on board to support my stepfather's brutal decade of raping and impregnating me. At least that is how it felt to me. Nobody believed me. McDarby's mantra haunted me still.

The next few weeks and months were not good at all. I went back to my doctor who put me on a course of anti-depressants and I tried to block out my emotions with the tablets and work. However, neither of them worked. I don't know if I was aware that I was pulling away from my family and friends. I didn't want to be with Karl anymore; I didn't want to be with the kids anymore and I didn't want to be in Ireland anymore. In my head I was drifting and no longer felt part of anything, though I continued to drive to and from Dublin for work.

My friend Norma travelled down from Belfast because she was so worried about me. Karl and I had befriended her on holidays and we had stayed in touch. She stayed overnight and then brought me back to Belfast the following day. I couldn't even dress for the journey, so I stayed in my pyjamas not saying a word to her. As far as I was concerned I had absolutely nothing to say to anyone. Over the next few days she fed me and did what she could for me. I was grateful to her for taking me away from the kids and Karl as I didn't want them to have to see how bad I really was.

At this stage Karl was working with Aware, travelling around Ireland to talk about suicide prevention. He may have been worried about me in this regard, but I was past the suicide stage. I could not have been bothered, since I would surely fail at it like everything else. I was putting myself back into that robotic state so that I would feel nothing. As a result I wanted to be alone and told Karl I wanted a separation. I was hardly talking to him. If he rang I just mumbled 'yes' or 'no' depending on whatever he was saying. I didn't feel like talking to him. I had to keep talking to the kids, of course, but it was the bare minimum required. They were all anxious about me, but I thought I was sparing them further worry by shutting down and refusing to talk about what I was going through.

The way I saw it was my relationship with Karl had been completely consumed by my years of trauma and abuse. All the consequences were there in our marriage and in the two sets of children we had. I needed to get away from it and, therefore, them. I stayed in the house in Monksfield and left Karl with the kids at home. We didn't say much to them, but I'm sure they worried terribly about us.

Judith, one of my best friends, was pregnant and I hardly saw her for the nine months since I decided it was better for everyone if I stayed away from them. At best I managed a few brief phone conversations, but that was about it.

I had disappeared to a dark place, making sure that nobody could follow me. Shame, guilt and remorse overwhelmed me with their familiarity. I also stopped eating and was rapidly shrinking. It really was like the old days. I got it into my head that I wanted to move to America. I hadn't worked out exactly where yet, but I was desperate to get out of Ireland. I looked up American colleges with a view to being a student and went as far as filling out forms, but then I ran out of steam.

Over those dark months I spoke infrequently to Karl and assumed that he was doing his best to make a life for himself without me. We had bought a second house for family holidays. I had fallen in love with it because it was an old Victorian house by the sea. However I was so bad that I could not even be bothered to go down and spend some time there. I wasn't the least bit interested in it or the sea. I really felt I was coming apart at the seams. Everyone else seemed the same, but I was going under and was convinced I was nothing, but a burden on my family and friends. I felt like a fuck-up, a total mess and, as usual, I was ashamed of my failings as a human being.

When Judith had her baby I forced myself to visit her and made arrangements with Karl to come with me as she was our mutual friend. I was burnt out and drastically underweight, so much so that I could only move slowly like an elderly or frail person. I had stopped taking the anti-depressants and I was bleeding pretty heavily. It was probably inevitable that I had to take some time off work. Karl hadn't seen me for a few weeks and was obviously shocked at the sight of me. When we got to Judith's she told him he should take me home again. Karl was angry over what I was doing to myself and upset over the separation, but I could not summon any feelings to care for him or what I was putting him through. In my head I was doing the best thing for everyone who cared about me, cutting myself off from them.

I went home with Karl and closed the curtains, not wanting anyone to see me, or me to see them. And that lasted about a year.

When I look back now, the best way I can describe it is that I went into hibernation. Karl and various friends fed me and looked after me, but I hardly noticed. Frequently, I watched myself from above and saw how I was wasting away. McDarby continued on with his normal life, while mine had ground to a halt. I retreated into what was left of my shell, just like a turtle. I have always loved turtles. In that way, I suppose I knew, on a certain level, that throughout all the darkness of those twelve months I was allowing healing to take place.

Those twelve months represent just about the worst and best period of my life. It was horrific, but it brought me to a different place inside of myself and today I still have the strength that I gathered from it. I spent many hours sitting on my sofa. I love books and am usually a voracious reader, but I could not concentrate on any book. I could not even focus on the television so I mostly just sat there in a daze, just like I used to do in Ardee.

Karl had been pushed to his limits and I understood this. For years he had worked so hard with me, showing infinite patience in teaching me to reach out and love, and be loved. Nevertheless he had not seen me this bad before and honestly felt I was too far gone for his help. He continued to worry that I was considering suicide and had the kids watch me, along with any number of our good friends. One day one of them paid me a visit. Seeing me on the sofa, my friend, who already has a loud booming voice, shouted at me, 'So you are just going to give up, Mary? Is that it?' I looked up at him and replied, 'Yeah. What do you want me to do?' He answered, 'I want you to get up for starters!' I shook my head, 'I don't have it in me!' That was pretty much the end of our conversation.

I stopped praying. I did not give a damn whether

there were angels around me or not. I saw and felt the distance from Karl, but had no idea how to bridge the gap. I certainly was beyond pretending to be anything other than me at possibly my lowest point ever. In fact that was something positive; I knew I was in a dark place. Years earlier, I had no idea how far gone I was. In this way it was like a spiritual awakening for me, with a new level of awareness being reached.

Iseult started talking about going to Australia and I knew why. Like Karl, she had reached the end of her tether and literally had run out of ideas to help me. She also wanted to escape the injustice of what had happened. I couldn't blame her. I could plainly see that the kids were worried. The twins were very young, but they knew there was something wrong with their mother, the woman who used to get into her car and drive to work and was usually a soft touch regarding their pocket money. Now she was spending her days just sitting on the sofa and staring into space.

But I do believe that this was all necessary despite the horribleness of that year. This actually was healing at a deep level. Shutting down for that bleak year allowed me to re-group, as it were, and gather my strength on an emotional, spiritual and mental level. At some point I began to pray again, even if I had not decided who exactly I was praying to. One day, when I was alone in the house, I lit four candles and sat myself down in the middle of my wooden floor and waited. I felt a scream inside of me and I let it out. It was a brief release and sounded more like a low guttural growl, but this was probably the first time that I had ever allowed myself to 'scream' and that was definitely a step in the right direction. A few minutes later I welcomed the knowledge that it was up to me to allow change to come in. As of yet, I had no idea how or when or what I was supposed to do, but trust seeped in that I would be guided towards it. Financially I was down to my last few pounds, but that was alright. I was ready to learn to crawl again before finding my feet and renewing my contact with my family, my friends and my world.

I realised that I had to forgive myself for what I had done to me and for what he had done to me. I had to stop carrying on his sabotage of me as a person. This surely was a hard lesson to learn, but it was one I could not easily forget. I could not go backwards anymore.

CHAPTER EIGHTEEN

My therapist always told me that I was a spiritual person. Years earlier I had worried that I was possessed, wondering if that was why I could see the dark shadows and feel spirits around me, but I was assured that no, this was just part of my spiritual being.

At some point I began to see a lot of hawks. I believe that everyone has spirit guides made up of all sorts of beings: angels, relatives that were long dead before you were born, people you did know who have passed on and, well, really anyone who has ever lived or died. Animals and birds can also be guides and I reckoned that hawks were one of my power animals. I am not looking to convert anyone, but this was simply how my life was developing. Alongside my work to 'fix' myself after years of abuse and the years of study I put into being the counsellor that I am today, I was also on a spiritual exploration, whether I liked it or not.

There are several meanings attached to the hawk as a spirit animal. All birds are recognised as messengers, but the hawk is the messenger of the spirit world and consequently has a strong connection with spirit. It carries the power of focus and clarity which allows it to take the lead when the time is right. When I began to see hawks in my meditation and dreams I felt it was a sign that my spiritual awareness was opening me up further and bringing me to another level.

It is hard to pinpoint this sort of stuff beyond saying that, at some stage, I began to develop an interest or an affinity with the Native American. I'm not sure if I can explain it any better except to say that I have been leaving stuff out along the way of this book. To be honest, I was unsure how to include it, but now I am going to make a stab at it.

Many, many years earlier I 'met' my first Native American. It was the night that I had messed up my face and tore up my clothes to help me prove to my mother that I had been raped. She didn't believe me so I raced back to my room to fix myself up before my stepfather came home and heard all about it. As I stood at the window, looking out at the traffic, and feeling completely forsaken, the face of an elderly man appeared out of the corner of my eye. His hair was long and white and his face was a busy map of wrinkles. He smiled and said four words to me, which were, 'Go to Wounded Knee!' And then he was gone again, just like that. Of course I believed I had imagined him, but I could never forget his message. About three years later I asked a teacher if she knew what 'Wounded Knee' was. She did some research and told me that it was in America and had been the site of a big battle.

Now we have to jump forward again, to an Alcoholics Anonymous (AA) world convention that took place in Toronto, Canada. Karl and I decided to go because several of our friends were going. I had always planned to go back to America because I felt I had unfinished business with the country and since Canada was right next door, this definitely felt like a step in the right direction.

Karl and I had been working hard and had saved some money. We asked our good friend to mind the children and off we went. Over the course of the convention I found an area inhabited by Native Americans and there was some sort of ceremony taking place. I was immediately hooked and felt that this was probably why I had come to Canada, and took the opportunity to get to know a few of them. There was just something about them, as a race, that I was drawn too, as if I had always known them. I felt I belonged.

Sometime after this I actually flew to America to attend an Native American convention and made more new friends. When I returned to Ireland I received a phone call from some Anishinaabe women I had met. They told me that they were thinking of coming to Ireland for a visit and wondered if they could call on me. I told them to come right over, that I would love to see them and show them around.

Thank goodness I have a big house because I had to put up eight women. They were Jingle Dancers from the Anishinaabe tribe from White Earth Ojibwe Reservation. The Jingle Dance is the women's 'pow wow' dance, in other words this is the dance performed by women at meetings and social gatherings (pow wows). They have a specific dress which is covered in rows of metal cones that jingle together like little bells. My friends wanted to perform their dance for anybody that might be interested in seeing it, because it is an important part of their culture and heritage, but there were no takers. So I contacted the twins' school and asked if I could bring the women in to perform for the children. Fortunately they agreed and it was a lovely visit. My friends did their dance while some of the children performed some Irish dancing in turn and learnt a little about the Anishinaabe culture. A local journalist also came by and wrote an article for the paper.

I had an instant connection with one of the women in particular. Like me, Jamie had led a tough life, but was doing her best to improve herself in order to learn to live her life free of undue influence from her past. She was sad to leave Ireland, confessing that she had felt very much at home here. On her last night we exchanged gifts; she gave me a little bear from her costume and I gave her a little angel figurine. We were like two halves of the same coin, she wanted to be Irish and I wanted to be Native American. We promised to keep in touch and, today, she is one of my very best friends.

She was able to tell me more about Wounded Knee. It is in South Dakota and, on 29 December 1890 was the scene of a horrific massacre by the US Calvary on the Lakota tribe. Most of the Lakota were unarmed and by the time the shooting stopped over two hundred Lakota men, women and children were dead, and a further forty-seven women and children were seriously wounded. Meanwhile twenty-five US soldiers died while twenty more were awarded the Medal of Honour for their murderous work that day in December. In 2001 the National Congress of American Indians condemned the awards and called on the American government to rescind them.

It would take me a few years, but I finally got there when Jamie and I arranged to do a spiritual trip around the USA. Some people go to Lough Derg or climb Croagh Patrick to do penance for their sins. It seemed like Wounded Knee was where I would commit to my own brand of penance and forgiveness of self.

I remember becoming emotional almost immediately. This was the place that had been calling to me since I was a little girl and it was hard to take in that I was finally here. The atmosphere was tremendous. The area had seen so much death and destruction and still the Native Americans had never given up. This was something I had in common with them. My stepfather had murdered a part of me, my innocence, and it was gone forever. Yet, for all that destruction of whom I had been or who I could have been if my father had not died so soon, I was still standing and, even more than that, I had made it to this sacred place.

The night before we had both made tobacco prayer ties, placing tobacco into bits of material for whomever you want to pray for. I made ties for Karl, the kids and all my ancestors. Jamie parked in the car park and I got out to read the tourist information on the enormous mountain that I could see in front of us. Most Native Americans believe that Bear Butte Mountain is a spiritual mountain because it is where their creator has chosen to communicate with them through visions and prayers. It is covered in any amount of prayer ties and visitors are asked not to touch or photograph them.

Out of the corner of my eye I saw Jamie put on her hiking boots. I was feeling hot and bothered and was also bleeding heavily. Suddenly feeling nervous, I asked her what she was doing. She looked aghast at such a stupid question, saying, 'Nobody comes out here to look at Bear Butte Mountain. You have to 'do' Bear Butte Mountain!' Weakly I mumbled something like, 'What?'

She answered, 'Mary, you have to climb the mountain as far as you can, and when you have reached your limit, you will see the right branch on which to place your prayer ties. That's how it works.'

I did not want to climb the mountain. I did not have any hiking boots with me. Furthermore, the closer we got to it the more I understood that this was by far the biggest mountain I had ever seen in my life. The sun was beating down on us and I felt exhausted already. However, I already understood it would be useless to attempt to thwart Jamie from making me follow her up that damn mountain.

We followed the age-old tracks that had been

made by those who had gone before us. The trail
was so narrow that we had to walk in single file, one
behind the other, which added to my sense of purpose
regarding this literal journey to the top of a steep
mountain. For me this represented my life to date.
Once I committed myself to the journey I started off
enthusiastically enough, wanting to 'do' Bear Butte
Mountain as much as Jamie. We took off at a strong
pace and for the first part it was fairly easy-going, all that
was required was to put one foot down after another,
but as we kept going I began to feel the journey was
growing in length and obstacles. I got tired and when
I looked back it seemed that we had not come as far
as I had imagined and there was still so much ground
to be covered. The more I focussed on the journey
ahead the more frequently I began to stumble over
rocks and tree trunks. After I don't know how long,
I began to despair as it looked as if we were still only
at the foot of the mountain. I had to drag mental and
physical strength out of me somehow and keep myself
motivated in mind and body. Step by step, that climb
turned into a metaphor for my life; I was determined
not to give up until it was time to. It helped not to
keep looking at what lay ahead of us. I had to keep
reminding myself to look around and concentrate on

where I was and not what still had to be done. In this way I began to notice the variety of shrubs and flowers which got me thinking about my grandmother and how much I still missed her after all these years.

As I continued, my head flooded with memories, most of them I would rather have forgotten, but there was no denying that as I climbed something was being released. My thoughts jumped back and forth from my childhood to my adolescence and then to my twenties, with various scenes replayed in my mind's eye. Out of the blue, I remembered McDarby's mother coming briefly to stay with us, in Ardee, just before she died, and telling my mother apologetically that she knew her son was a 'bad one'. I remembered that big Native American telling me to go back to Ireland, after I found out the kids had been taken into care. Had he really existed? And then look at what happened the day I arrived home. Thank God I had no idea of what lay ahead of me after I got off the plane at Dublin airport. However, it wasn't all bad. I felt Karl, my soulmate, beside me, matching me step for step. In reality he was back home in Ireland with the kids, but I felt his support in spirit. I could hear him telling me how proud he was of me. I also felt the kids around me urging me to keep going. I felt loved on that mountain in a way I had possibly never appreciated before.

On I plodded, Jamie just ahead of me. The sweat was rolling down my back. There had been a fire on the mountain a while before, and burnt stumps that were once glorious trees dotted the route. It struck me that they also mirrored my inner being in that they were still here having stood strong against a fiery destruction. As hard as it was and as awful as I felt, I could not deny the feeling that what I was doing felt absolutely right and true. This battered mountainside in South Dakota made me feel more at home than any corner of Ardee.

Every so often we stopped to drink water from Jamie's backpack. Our conversation had long ground to a halt as we both concentrated on our own climb and gave ourselves over to the reasons we were doing this. We were two separate women sharing a pathway for an individual experience.

Thinking about my grandmother, I reflected on how she had done her best to help me and had tried to pass on her knowledge of plants and herbs. Why hadn't I listened to her and taken notes? After about two and a half hours I felt I was in dire straits and was unsure if I could continue. Jamie showed no sign of slowing down which prevented me from stopping.

She was ahead of me and, from time to time, would look back to check my progress. I needed help of some sort. Suddenly I felt my grandmother around me and I heard a gentle voice inside my head tell me to chew on some sage. I had spied sage plants all around me and gratefully plucked some leaves and popped them in my mouth. This miracle of a plant is famous for its healing properties and is regarded as a tonic for the likes of stomach problems, headaches, the kidney, liver, sexual organs and so on. It can be used internally and externally and the Native Americans used to mix it with bear grease to treat open wounds.

I kept going for another while, wishing a bathroom would suddenly appear so that I could wash myself and change my sanitary towel. In the heat I could just about smell the sweetness of my own blood and I hated feeling so dirty and sweaty. It had been a while since Jamie had looked around and the distance had slowly grown between us. Not wanting to shout at her to stop, I stared at her back and silently begged her to turn around. She did, allowing me to indicate to her that I felt that I had reached my limit. I was not impressed when she pointed to a ledge up ahead of her, in the distance, and gestured that she would wait for me there.

It took me at least another fifteen minutes to reach her and for those fifteen minutes I prepared myself to angrily state my case – that she had not warned me I would be climbing a mountain and, therefore, I was not wearing hiking boots, like she was. Furthermore, I was bleeding heavily and felt I was on the verge of collapse. My anger and self-righteousness was probably what kept me going until I reached her ledge. Fortunately when I opened my mouth to make my speech, nothing would come out. I was too exhausted.

Oblivious to the lecture that she had narrowly missed, Jamie held out her hands to catch mine, looked deep into my eyes and said, 'I love you. You are so important to me and I will hold you in my heart forever.' Next she placed a prayer tie in my hand. Tears blinded me. I knew she had spoken from her heart and I felt that she could see the real me. I had not shared my entire story with her, but, at that moment, I felt she had read my journey to this place at this time. We both cried. For the first time in my life I could imagine what it was like to have a sister. Jamie was a kindred spirit, in that she could see beyond the mask I presented to the world, and yet she still loved me. I felt a wondrous peace settle inside me and then I knew I had arrived at the spot where I would find the right branch for me.

I gazed around me and spotted a branch whose life had been extinguished in the fire. It was dead yet it remained here, a no-longer living testament to the fire and everything else it had weathered in its life, with its scorched wounds on display. I knew at once that this was the branch for me, that this was exactly where I would place my prayer ties. As I reached up to it, I felt renewed and as I placed my little packages in its embrace, I saw at once how beautiful the branch was, only noting now how it hung out over the ledge I was sitting on before stretching further out to overlook the plains below me. Yes, this was where I could leave behind my deepest pain and this was where I would place my blessings and wishes for those I loved. This would be *my* sacred place for my darkness and my light.

As I cried I knew I was being cleansed on a spiritual level. I knew I had served my penance and that I deserved to be standing in this particular spot on Bear Butte Mountain. I knew that this was also about forgiving myself. That was the key to happiness for whatever life I had left on this earth; I would have to forgive myself.

I also knew that I wanted to keep going until I reached the top of the mountain.

Jamie and I looked at one another in silence and then we readied ourselves for the rest of the journey. On our way up we met plenty of people on their way back down again. I wondered about their lives and their reasons for making this pilgrimage. The climb grew quite dangerous the higher we went. One slip and I could have fallen off the side of the mountain, but this felt appropriate to the experience. I clung on and kept going. I felt a new energy build and my body felt lighter and more flexible. I thought about everyone: Karl, the kids, my parents, my friends and my stepfather. I suppose it was like a meditation in its own way, without any distractions to pull me away from it.

Almost five hours after we left the car I could see the top, and then something caught my eye. I watched in awe as an eagle soared above me and circled the mountain's peak. What a sight! This was the bird that flew higher than any other. The Native Americans believe that the eagle carries prayers on its wings to the creator. It was a magical moment for me and I felt that my prayers and blessings had been heard. I took a well-earned break, recognising that a shift had taken place within me. I could not have said what it was, but I felt different. Lighting some of the sage, I swished it about me to cleanse my energy of any old negativity that dared to linger.

A breeze struck up through the trees around me and I saw hundreds, if not thousands, of prayer ties swaying in amongst the leaves. Scrambling over some boulders I found an eagle's feather, the perfect souvenir for the climb. I don't think I can fully describe my sense of accomplishment as I stood at the top. Jamie had wandered off and I had plenty of time to take in my surroundings and give thanks and praise for the help and love I had received that had helped finally get me here. I had done it.

I had 'done' Bear Butte Mountain, all four miles of it.

CHAPTER NINETEEN

When I returned home, McDarby's health began to disintegrate. My stepfather was experiencing blackouts and loss of memories. He was finally diagnosed with Lewy Body Dementia (LBD), which was like a cross between dementia and Parkinson's disease. When it flared up he would be hunched over and unable to flex his muscles and limbs and would also be confused about his surroundings. I could not help thinking that this was his punishment for the life he had lived.

James was the one trying to deal with him and I knew he was struggling. Following one of McDarby's hospital visits his doctor called the family together for a meeting. Mother was drunk in Ardee, leaving James, Karl and me to work out a solution regarding full-time care for my stepfather. I could not leave James to manage him alone so we decided Karl and I would bring him back to Ardee and that we would take turns to check in on the both of them. So the hospital released McDarby into our car, and we drove to Ardee. When we brought him into the house Mother was completely out of it and McDarby didn't seem to understand where he was. We left him standing in a daze while we went back outside to talk, both feeling that we could not simply drive away.

Karl rang the hospital for ideas on what to do next. Of course the hospital explained that since they had released the patient, he was no longer in their care. However, it was suggested that we find a home for him, but Karl and I knew nothing about homes and, also, it was now late in the evening and too late to start organising anything. Karl asked about McDarby's family, but I had no numbers for any of them, and besides, I didn't think my stepfather had had much if any contact with them over the previous years. Briefly we considered bringing him to his house in Carlow, but we knew that the building was derelict. So, what did that leave us with?

I cannot remember which one of us suggested it first, that we bring him back to our house. We both worked in the caring profession and found it impossible to leave him in such a state with his wife who wasn't much better. Neither of us wanted to take him home, but we were caught between a rock and a hard place. Believe me, we both wanted to walk away and climb into our car and disappear … but we couldn't. Karl asked me if I thought it would be safe to bring him home. We believed he was a paedophile and we had our children's safety to think about. However we had to admit that physically he was much too frail and bewildered to harm anyone. If we put him in the log cabin we would not need to take him into the house. His meals would be brought out to him and the doctor could check up on him in the cabin.

It was an awful decision, but we felt that, as human beings, we had no choice. We must have been outside for maybe thirty minutes, but when we went back inside, McDarby was still standing in the exact spot we had left him, his head drooped and his back hunched over. Mother was in a drunken stupor. We packed some clothes for him and rang home to ask the kids if they were okay with us taking him in. They told us to do whatever we felt was best. I asked them to turn on the heating in the cabin and make up a bed for him.

The drive home was a quiet one. I guess both Karl and I were deep in thought. I admitted to myself that I felt sorry for this senile old man, who I managed to separate from the monster that almost destroyed me. When we got home, Karl assured me that he alone would perform the physical care which we both knew meant changing his nappies, dressing him, feeding him and washing him. I could not have brought myself to do any of that while Karl was adamant that he did not want me near him. And so it was that over the next few weeks, Karl nursed my stepfather back to health.

We did not expect him to improve, but that was the nature of his particular illness. It was quite a difficult and unsettling situation. Karl treated McDarby as a normal patient and extended to him all the necessary care that was required, which resulted in McDarby getting better and stronger ... which resulted in him returning to his old self, the monster. Karl hated him and hated having him around. Meanwhile as McDarby got better, I began to go downhill. I hated having him there too. I was worried about the children and also began to succumb to the most horrific of memories. When he was strong enough he began to leave his cabin and actually walk into our house – clearly something that neither Karl nor I had foreseen. Karl was caught between feeling proud that he had nursed someone back from death's door and sensing that the situation was no longer a safe one.

I actually wondered if McDarby would apologise for what he had done to me. Would he want to try and make it up to me? Furthermore I wanted him to see how great my life was now. Could he understand that I was a much-loved wife and mother? Did he notice how happy my children were and that our home was a contented one? However he was blind to it all. He also neglected to thank Karl for the weeks of caring for him and acted as if it was only his due. Karl was losing himself to his hatred for this man and decided to confront him with the past. He asked McDarby why and how he could have treated me like that; McDarby replied that he could not explain any of it, but did marvel at the fact that I had managed to survive it. He said he was sorry … as if that was enough to erase ten years of systematic rape and abuse. Then Karl asked him if we could trust him to stay away from our girls. Without thinking, McDarby answered, 'Ah, sure you wouldn't get away with it today. Kids are too clever, they'd only tell on me. Anyway I would never touch blood!'

So this was the only assurance he could provide that he would not touch the girls.

I wanted to kill him. I felt sick to my soul, but somehow I managed not to betray myself. Karl kept himself together too, only asking McDarby if he missed my mother. When McDarby said yes, Karl told him to get his stuff together, because he would drive him to Ardee the following morning to see her. McDarby agreed to this, believing that he would just be paying a visit. Halfway through the drive he must have realised the truth and begged Karl not to leave him in Ardee. Karl ignored his pleading. That morning we had promised one another that McDarby would never step foot in our home ever again. Once more my stepfather had showed his true colours. There was no point in hoping that he would change or be influenced by goodness. He was evil through and through and would always be as long as he felt strong enough. I had phoned Mother so she was expecting him and was only a little bit drunk when Karl dropped her husband off. Later that evening he rang to beg Karl to come and get him. Karl told him that he was no longer welcome and that he was where he belonged: in Ardee, with his wife.

It took me a week to recover from this. When I was ready I burnt sage throughout the entire house, expelling all the bad energy and clearing out the atmosphere. Sage is like incense; you light it and then quickly blow it out, letting the smell and its wisp of smoke do the work. Meanwhile Karl re-decorated and only then did we feel we had returned to normal. Our house was once more our home where we felt loved and at peace.

CHAPTER TWENTY

I tried my best with my mother, but to no avail. Her body was starting to crumble from the years of alcohol abuse, and emotionally and mentally she was in poor shape too. Therefore, she was unable to communicate in a meaningful way and our meetings usually involved me giving her money that I knew she would probably use to buy more drink. I never wanted to talk to her when she was drunk because that usually led to an argument, since I found it impossible not to berate her for drinking.

As some point I told her I was attending AA meetings and begged her to come with me. She came with me just once or twice, but stormed out every time because she neither wanted to listen to others talk about their addiction nor discuss hers with anyone else. Two friends of mine from AA agreed to pay her a visit in Ardee. I hoped they might reach her in a way that I could not. However they reported back to me that she was too full of pride to admit to having a problem, and furthermore, they both genuinely felt that she was too far gone now and would never stop drinking.

I made that hundred-mile drive to Ardee as frequently as I could to check on her and to beg her to reduce her alcoholic intake if she could not give it up. I did all I could in between work, study and my own family, but it was disheartening to drive all the way up there and find her too drunk to talk to. It upset me that my children had no relationship with her. I brought them a couple of times, but the visit would usually disintegrate into her crying in front of them and saying over and over again to me, I'm sorry, I'm sorry!' I had heard those words so many times over the last thirty years or so. As far as I was concerned it was blatant self-pity; she had no idea how her behaviour affected those around her, only how it affected herself.

The hospital would ring to say she was back with them and either Karl or I would drive up to give her a nightdress and shampoo and a litre bottle of 7Up. She took to signing herself back out again after we said goodbye, the doctors unable to convince her to stay put. God – how I hated going to see her in the ward and smelling the drink off her. I found it hard to listen to her tearful apologies when her breath reeked of alcohol.

When she eventually got too bad to leave the hospital

my stepfather, whose health was also in decline, was in another ward. Oh, how she worried about him. At one point Karl had asked Mother who her big love had been – Daddy or McDarby – and she had readily answered that McDarby had been the true love of her life. It did not make any sense to me.

As it happened, McDarby thought he was dying. Karl and I went to his room to check up on him and agreed that he looked like a dying man. When he spoke he didn't make any sense and he was in an extremely weakened state. Karl wondered if he had lost his memory too and had already left behind the evil life he had lived. On the other hand, maybe he remembered everything and was now ready to confess. Thanks to my mother's frequent stays we had got to know the priest who worked in the hospital. Karl spotted him in the corridor and, introducing himself as McDarby's son-in-law, he pretended to be concerned about McDarby's soul in the afterlife and asked the priest if he would visit McDarby to hear his confession. The priest willing agreed, but what exactly would McDarby confess to? We knew the priest would not be able to disclose what was said in confession.

The priest heard my stepfather's confession and went as far as confiding in Karl that McDarby had confessed to him. Karl hesitated and then told the priest that McDarby had raped and abused his stepdaughter for years. The priest interrupted him to explain that he had had a couple of chats with McDarby and he knew what he did to his stepdaughter and he knew about the children. He added, 'Without breaking my vows I can assure you that Sean has made a *full* confession.' Karl pretended he was happy to please the obliging priest, but, at heart, he was livid that McDarby was going to die in peace, as far as his mortal soul was concerned. For my part I wondered at the ease of it, to simply be absolved of rape and abuse following a few minutes with the priest. In any case, he didn't die and, who knows, maybe that was his punishment. God knows he had little left to live for at this point.

Some months later Karl and I had taken the kids away for a holiday when the nurse rang to tell me that Mother was very bad. We cut short our break and hurried to her side. However by the time we got there she was on the mend once more. In fact she was released some time after, but first she had to meet with her doctor. We went with her. He informed us that if she took care of herself she might well live for another fifteen or twenty years, but if she had as much as one more glass of wine he predicted that she would not see out the end of the year.

Following some discussion Karl and I agreed to take her home with us. Karl was so reliable like that. Although I recognised that it was too late to have the mother I wanted, I felt that this could be the perfect opportunity for some sort of healing for her and for our relationship. And Karl was generous enough to agree to accommodate my hopes and her. Mother also agreed to this and so this rather huge decision was quickly made. We had to drive her home to Ardee to get more clothes and whatever else she wanted to bring with her. Unfortunately once we reached the house and she got out of the car, she changed her mind, insisting she was staying in Ardee. Rightly or wrongly I grew angry with her, telling her we were doing our best to help her. Of course I knew why she wouldn't come home with us. She knew that I would not allow her to drink and, therefore, could not go through with it. I had hoped she could fight the addiction and spend some relatively quality time with me and her grandchildren, but she only wanted to drink. It was as simple as that.

Karl brought her suitcase into the kitchen as she roared at us. Next she went to her bedroom to retrieve a bottle of vodka. In other words it was time for us to leave. It was upsetting, but we were utterly powerless to do anything about her drinking. She did not want to stop and refused to even try. On the drive home I thought back to years earlier when she ended up in Saint John of God's Hospital. Rikki and I were only kids and the doctors told her out straight that she was an alcoholic. She mutely accepted their diagnosis and turned it into the perfect excuse to keep drinking. She was an alcoholic and, therefore, there was nothing to be done for her. Of course it was not her fault that she had to keep drinking, because she was an alcoholic and this is what alcoholics do. This was her justification to keep drinking.

Memories swamped me. How many times had Rikki and I had to physically hold on to her to prevent her from jumping out of a moving car? I remembered James's miserable Confirmation Day that she ruined and then there was the time she had left him in the shopping centre in Dundalk and was oblivious to the fact she had lost him until the guards knocked at the door. Alcohol ruled and ruined her life, and ours too for that matter.

Over the next few months we had to retrace our steps to the hospital many times as she and McDarby were both taken in, cared for and then released again.

It was a tough year and Karl and I decided that we would take another family holiday. A few days before we were due home we received one more phone call. Mother was back in hospital and this time I knew it was the end. I stood there and asked the angels for strength to get me through this final stage. As I prayed to them a tiny pink flower fell into my hand. Take my word for it – I was nowhere near any flowers or trees. Karl smiled at me and said, 'The angels are sending their love to you.' I took it as a sign that I would be okay.

As soon as we got home we quickly unpacked the car before driving straight to the hospital. Mother's condition was extremely poor and two days later she was on life support. The nurse rang me and asked that the family come in for a meeting. Rikki said he would meet us there. Karl and I picked up James and when we got to the hospital we found my stepfather sitting outside her room. He was quite senile by now and didn't seem to know where he was. He just kept saying that Mother had been eating cherries and that he had had to tell her to stop eating them. She had mouth ulcers, which resulted in her frequently vomiting blood and in his confused state he thought she had been eating cherries.

The doctor met with us and advised that there was no hope for her, and that she would most likely die within thirty minutes or so of the machines being switched off. She was unconscious now.

Karl led McDarby in so that he could hold his wife's hand for a few minutes, but he was too far gone to understand what was going on, so Karl brought him back outside. James found it too difficult to watch her die so he stayed outside with his father while Karl and I went in to sit with her. I held her hand and noticed all the different coloured bruises up and down her arm, the result of her many falls over the last year or so. Somehow I felt she knew I was there and had been waiting for me even though she never opened her eyes. The nurses came in and asked if I was ready to have the machines turned off. I nodded and they asked us to leave the room while they did this. A couple of minutes later I was allowed back in again. She looked like she was fast asleep.

It felt right that I should be the last one with her. I told her that I forgave her for not being the mother that I wanted and needed and that she was free to go as soon as she felt ready. I also told her that I knew life had been hard for her and I hoped she was going to a better place where she would find the peace that she had never had here on earth. I couldn't help thinking that her life had been an awful waste. Within moments her body was gone, I knew that, but I felt her spirit linger to listen to me. I rubbed her hand as I waited for it to leave, not wanting to move until I was sure it was gone. Then I went outside to tell the rest of them that she had passed. My brother looked sad, he had never known her as a proper mother either, while McDarby just looked lost and confused. I remember thinking it could all have been so different. Karl arranged for cups of tea and coffee and had us brought to an empty room.

It was the end of an era.

The funeral director asked me to fetch some clothes for Mother to wear since all she had on her was the hospital gown. Karl drove me to the house and parked in the driveway. The place was desolate. We walked by rusted cars with weeds sprouting from them including Mother's red Jaguar, which was covered in rust, its windows smashed, and seemed to be feeding a mini jungle of its own. The back door was falling apart, a piece of wood covering the gap left by the missing window. Inside, the kitchen was still dominated by engines and unidentifiable ancient car parts while the floor was streaked with oil. There was so much stuff all over the place that I could hardly see the table in the corner. The doors of the lilac presses were open. Once they had been full of expensive cups and plates, but now I only saw one or two cups. The items that had made this a home – in those early days before McDarby had showed up – were long gone.

I made my way to Mother's bedroom, doing my best to ignore the appalling smell in it. Opening her wardrobe door I gazed at the different outfits, suddenly remembering how beautiful she used to be. She had once spent a fortune on how she looked and would never tolerate so much as a stray hair. What had happened to that woman? Surely she was in a better place now.

Karl arranged everything. At the funeral home McDarby sat in the corner with his sister. Nobody else went near him and I couldn't help feeling sorry for him. The funeral took place in Ardee which made it all the more difficult. Being a small town, lots of people turned up and I tried to ignore my paranoia that they knew about me or bits about me and that was what they had come out to see. In fact, some of my mother's family approached me to say stuff about McDarby and my younger self, but I could not listen to them. It was too little, too late and, besides, it was hardly the time to reminisce about such things.

At the removal, McDarby and his sister sat together at the back of the church. My brothers, Karl, the kids and I were all up front. McDarby was not mentioned at all in the service and, the following day, he didn't turn up for the funeral.

Karl bought white roses for me and Mother's siblings to throw into the grave before it was closed. Mother's family stepped forward, threw in their rose and said their own private farewells. One of them said, as she passed by me, 'I hope McDarby is not going to be buried there because that's my mother's grave.' I didn't say anything to her, wondering how it was only now that she was worried about him. How easy it was to make a stand now.

It was a sad, sad day.

A few weeks later my Mother gave me a final kick from the grave. Rikki rang to tell me that she had made no mention of me in the will and had left everything to himself and James. James went to the solicitor to explain that her husband was still alive and so was entitled to something too. They will was amended and the estate was divided between the three of them. Once more my mother showed me how little I had counted. The man who had abused me was now going to get a share of the house that my father had built. As far as I was concerned, this killed any last hope that I had scraped together that she might have loved me even a little bit.

On a spiritual level I had reached the conclusion that from the very beginning, McDarby must have been a sick man. To have inflicted what he did on me for all those years had to mean that mentally he had never been well. One day I watched a film about a girl who had been abused. She was American and had found out about a safe house that was on the other side of the country. In other words it was, in her opinion, far enough from her abuser so that she could believe it would keep her safe. She set out with very little money and, on reaching the house, was given a room of her own. Her door was alarmed which meant that nobody could access the room or sneak in without her knowledge and therefore she felt completely safe. She could not speak to her rescuers and tell them what she had gone through. The only evidence was the length of the journey she had made to reach them. I completely identified with her and was in tears as it ended because it took me so long to find my safe place.

I had to have my womb removed. I had been plagued by heavy bleeding for years and it was gradually draining me of energy and good health. God only knows how much I spent on visiting different doctors. I was put on umpteen tablets to see if the bleeding could be reduced or stopped, but nothing worked for me. The truth was that I had been neglecting myself for years. My relationship with food was still problematic though Karl and I were working on that. It was rare for me to feel hungry, but we grew our own potatoes and vegetables and when I was feeling low Karl would make me his nutritious pumpkin soup. I had been suffering from migraines, but found that when I started to eat more regularly they all but vanished. A smear test revealed abnormal cells that had to be burned off.

Because I had such a high tolerance for pain I managed to ignore the heavy bleeding for about four years before I ended up in the Coombe having my womb taken out. I was unprepared for how emotional I was about this. For years I had absolutely hated that part of my body and now it was being taken out of me just as I had learned to love and appreciate it. I understood that the loss of blood had made me anaemic and unwell for as long as I could remember. When the kids were younger I had never been sick, but over the last few years I frequently succumbed to flu, chest infections and was never in the whole of my health. My body was telling me that it had had enough.

It was like my womb was grieving through blood in place of tears, for all those years of rape and violence. They didn't take out my ovaries, so I didn't have to deal with an instant menopause on top of everything else. Nevertheless, the operation was a difficult one and, months later, I was still in some pain. Furthermore I was quite low in myself. When I returned to work six weeks later I was still upset over losing that part of me.

CHAPTER TWENTY-ONE

About eight months after the reading of the will McDarby took ill again and was admitted to hospital in Drogheda. Once more the family was summoned by the doctor to discuss the situation. James asked me to be there so Karl and I drove to Drogheda. James had also contacted one of McDarby's brothers who turned up. Before the meeting Karl, and I went to see McDarby in his ward. He was semi-conscious and I felt that he was near the end. We took the lift to the doctor's office and found that James and his uncle were there before us. McDarby's brother said nothing as we took our seats. The doctor described the condition of his patient and asked if Karl and I could take care of him again. Before we could make a reply, the brother piped up, 'Why would you leave him with them since they hardly kept him a week the last time?' Naturally Karl reared up, 'I'm sorry?' The brother obliged by explaining to all of us how Karl and I had 'dumped' his poor brother in Ardee to fend for himself.

Karl addressed the doctor, 'It was his wife that I left him with, at his own home, in Ardee!' Next he addressed the brother, 'And whatever issues you have about that, this is not the time to discuss them.' Normally I would have left Karl to deal with this, but I felt a new rage which enabled me to add, 'You have no idea of what has gone on here. He was very lucky that we even took him for the few weeks. Now, unless you would like me to go into details in front of the doctor, I'd suggest that you stay quiet. And, by the way, where have you been all these years? You're just popping up now at the end. Are *you* taking him to live with you? Well, are you?'

To be honest, I'm not entirely sure today that I actually said all of that. In any case the brother froze and did not utter another word, leaving as soon as the meeting was over. It was decided that McDarby would remain in hospital until he was a little better, not that he was expected to get much better again. Once he improved he would be transferred to a home in Louth. His brother wasn't around the day that McDarby had to be driven there. It was left to James, Karl and me to help get him settled although there was not much for us to do. At the home, the staff showed us his new room and the facilities, but I had no interest in any of it. The home was more than he deserved. I watched as the nurses treated him kindly and I had to remind myself that in their eyes he was just a frail old man in ill health. Karl fought the temptation to tell them the truth.

A few months later, I felt I needed to put him to rest in my soul and asked Karl and James to accompany me. I believed that this would be the last time that I would see him alive. On reaching his room I heard him labour to breathe. I hoped that this visit would also help James as I was sure he needed to make his peace with him too. James spent a few minutes with him and then left me alone with him. I opened my mouth and the words flowed. I told him that it was not my job to forgive him because he would be meeting his Maker soon enough and would have to earn His forgiveness there. I reminded him how he had left four children without a father on their birth certificate, not to mention the fifth child who had been taken away for adoption. I told him he had never given me a chance and that he should have gone to jail, but he was too much of a coward to face up to his actions of destruction. 'It is so easy to possess women and children, to bully and torment them with evil. Well, that same evil is running through your veins now!'

When I finished he opened his eyes and looked straight at me. I knew his spirit had heard every word and I experienced a wave of satisfaction. It was something I had to do, a verbal release after years of being told to keep my mouth shut. Holding my head up high, I walked out of that room without as much as a backward glance.

None of the children wanted to see him.

Some time later I woke up suddenly, my heart pounding. It was 3am on the morning of 19 December 2009 and I felt like somebody had kicked me. I was winded and my chest felt thick and heavy. I was gasping to breathe and then my entire body shuddered. Next I felt a tremendous heat as if hot water was spilling over my head, but before I could concentrate on that I saw a burst of colour, vibrant purples and greens, at the end of the bed. Had I entered another dimension? I knew I was awake and that I was in bed and that Karl was fast asleep beside me, but what else was going on? And then I knew in my heart and soul that it was my stepfather. I could not speak so I could not cry out to Karl and when I tried to push him awake I found I was paralysed.

The room filled with a bitter, rancid smell that made me gag. Then, as I lay perfectly still, not out of choice, I felt McDarby's spirit enter every cell, starting at the crown of my head and working its way down like a needle sewing a thread into a cushion. I was dripping in sweat and quickly alternated between being boiling hot and freezing cold. Of course I was scared, but I also realised that something important was happening. In fact I knew exactly what was going on. McDarby must be dying and this was the last act of his troubled spirit, piercing my every cell to experience what he had put me through, needing to feel my pain and my trauma. He was meeting his Maker and had to bring with him all that he had done in this life in order to be forgiven.

Part of me was awestruck by what was happening while another part succumbed to an overwhelming grief and horrendous sorrow. Was this his sorrow or mine? Gradually I felt him take his leave of me as the colours subsided and my temperature returned to normal. A single solitary tear rolled down my face and I definitely felt his spirit pass on.

As soon as I could talk and move again I shook Karl awake and told him what had happened, but he was too sleepy to respond and quickly fell back asleep. I tried to wake him up again and was making a third attempt when my phone rang. Even as I reached for it I knew. I answered it and heard James say, 'Mary, he's dead.'

It was a strange day that followed the phone call. Karl was ecstatic that McDarby was gone although he did his best to hide his feelings of relief and elation from me. As the kids got up, one by one, we told them. They all had their own reactions and I was glad that they felt free enough to express them to me. It was over at last. James turned up and offered to help with the arrangements. Karl rang an undertaker while James carried out the more personal aspects, fetching clothes for his father to wear in the coffin.

There was one more thing that I needed to do. Thinking back over my experience of having my fear and trauma absorbed by my stepfather's spirit, I knew there was one piece from that decade of darkness that he had missed out on. He was lucky enough to have a coffin and family to organise a funeral while one of his children had been quickly and silently buried in a field in Carlow. I had told the guards about that child when I was making my statement. They told McDarby to show them where he had buried the baby and I knew he had purposely brought them elsewhere because neither the body nor the material he had wrapped it in was ever found.

I explained to Karl and Iseult what I wanted to do and asked them if they felt they could accompany me to the field. They both said yes and we set off. On the drive I let my mind wander, thinking about the passing years, this lost child, Andrew and the rest of my children who only wanted to be there for me. How lucky I was now in many ways.

Since it was so close to Christmas the funeral was organised to take place in a couple of days, but I was damned if McDarby was meeting his Maker alone. This tiny innocent had lain in the cold field, without an attending priest or headstone, for years and years, but now I could ensure that his father would finally do right by him. McDarby was going to have to face up to every act that he had committed against me. I was not going to let him get away scot free even if everyone else did.

Karl parked the car and I got out. It was a cold morning and the ground beneath my feet was frozen solid. I had to walk across several fields to reach the one I wanted. Years earlier he had given me a sketchy description of whereabouts the body was and I felt myself being led to the spot. I took out the small garden fork that I had brought with me and, getting down on my hunkers, began to dig until I reached the clear soil. Next I took out my hanky, scooped up a handful of earth into it from my baby's burial plot and blessed it.

Later that day Karl drove me to the funeral home where McDarby was lying in state, in his coffin. We had to wait until the room cleared out. As soon as it was safe to, I opened up the lower part of the coffin and placed the handkerchief of earth into his pocket: the final piece of my story, never to be forgotten.

AFTERWORD

It is interesting to observe the 'coincidences' in one's life – how certain things seem to happen at just the right time. My daughter Iseult lived in Australia for three and a half years and I was fortunate to be able to visit her twice. By the time I boarded the plane in Dublin Airport for my second visit, in January 2014, two significant events had occurred. Firstly, I had become a grandmother, which rocked me emotionally and mentally. I wasn't prepared for the feelings of joy and the conflicting feelings of envy and jealousy that I experienced over the simple fact that my daughter had me to help. I reluctantly relived all those early pregnancies that I had experienced by myself without a friendly helping hand until Karl came into my life.

Secondly, thanks to Rikki, I had found contact details for my father's relatives who had emigrated to Australia in the 1960s. Aside from Aunt Josie, I had lost contact with all of them. However one of my few memories about them involved a cousin calling out to the house. I was about fourteen years old at the time and got a huge shock on answering the front door to find someone the image of my father standing on the doorstep. I worked up the courage to contact them and they arranged a reunion so that I got to meet Dad's nieces and nephews. In fact I discovered that my father's brother was still alive and living in New Zealand.

It turned out that Josie had told her sisters and brother some stuff about what was happening. I told my cousins a bit more and it seemed I was merely confirming what they already knew. We didn't dwell on the past as I didn't want my visit to be mired in the ugly reality of my past. It was wonderful to be surrounded by this loving extended family; it felt like I had come home again. They did confirm that they tried to get Grandma to come out for a visit after my grandfather had died, but she refused to leave Rikki and me and so the plane tickets were never used.

***

Last Friday I went to my school reunion in Ardee. I had Karl drive me there because I knew this was going to be a big deal. The girl who organised it had told me to text her when I was outside the bar so that she could come out to get me. She told me the others were looking forward to seeing me which only made me more nervous.

Karl dropped me outside and drove on to Rikki's flat where we would be spending the night. I texted my friend and she appeared immediately, giving me a hug and leading me inside. I hardly recognised anyone and battled my shyness and anxiety about what they remembered about me and my family. It was unclear as to who knew what, but I did my best to chat and smile. Of course I was wearing my 'armour' of make-up, designer outfit and designer shoes.

At some point my discomfort grew and I texted Karl to join me. Afterwards a few of us returned to my friend's house for an hour or so. I drank tea while the others had wine. When I got up to leave, my friend invited me to come back the next morning for breakfast.

I only got to sleep about 3am, but was wide awake four hours later. The flat was quiet; Rikki and Karl were still out cold. I got up and made myself a cup of tea. My head was awash with memories and the strangeness of being back in Ardee. When Karl got up he knew I was in a fragile state.

We headed back to my friend's house at midday, where I learned a great deal. One of the girls at breakfast told me, 'What I remember most, Mary, is that you had no friends, but you had plenty of money and probably nobody else knew that you used to give me and a few others money whenever we needed it. People talked about your pregnancy, but they didn't know about your generosity. I also remember that when we walked home from school I'd have to stop down the road because you were not allowed to walk with anyone. If we passed you on the road and your step-father was nearby you used to put your head down.' She paused and added, 'and I remember your poor grandfather walking up and down outside your house, holding up the sign that his grandchildren were being abused.'

It was not easy to listen to any of this, but I knew it was why I had agreed to come to the reunion, which was certainly timely considering I had just about finished writing this book. It seemed to me that before I could put the final full stop on this manuscript I had to first return home. It was always something that had worried me, how I had been thought of in my home town.

My stomach lurched as she told me that when I was pregnant the second time her mother had ordered her to stay away from me. The general consensus was that

I had taken McDarby away from my mother. Some woman had said this to her mother who had said it to her. My friend talked about seeing the light go out of my eyes.

I felt nauseous and excused myself to go outside for a minute. I was also angry. He had taken away my childhood and taken away my home. And everyone had believed that I was the one in the wrong, not my stepfather nor my mother.

When I went back inside, another friend said that she had met me once in Dundalk when I had all the children with me. It must have been when I was trying to get them back. I told her I could not remember seeing her and she nodded, saying that I had seemed completely gone in myself.

After breakfast Karl and I returned to Rikki's flat to collect our things. It really had been a rollercoaster ride, but I was glad to have reconnected with my friends and we hugged one another goodbye, promising not to leave it so long the next time.

At the flat Rikki handed me a piece of paper on which he had written, 'I'm sorry I could not protect you as I heard your screams on the wind and in my dreams'. That was it. I went into the bathroom and broke down. He followed me and held me as my body shook, sobbing for that innocent auburn-haired girl who I had hated and had blamed for everything. I had turned my back on her years ago, but now – *now* – I understood all that she had gone through and saw that it was not her fault.

It was not her fault.

HEALTH BOARD

Summary Report on
Mary Manning

Health Board

SUMMARY REPORT ON MARY MANNING

The case of Mary Manning and the welfare of her four children: Rory, Ashley, Iseult and Andrew was referred to me in August 1987 by ▇▇▇▇▇▇ Senior Social Worker and ▇▇▇▇▇▇ Social Worker, ▇▇▇▇▇▇▇▇▇▇▇▇. Mary had departed for the U.S.A. and the four children were residing with their maternal grandmother Mrs Mona Mc Darby at Ardee, Co. Louth. In October 1987, I placed Ashley, Iseult and Andrew in fostercare.

In 1988, I assisted ▇▇▇▇▇▇▇▇▇ Adoption Society in the placement of Andrew for adoption. In the above arrangements, I was assisted by ▇▇▇▇▇▇▇▇▇▇ Social Worker, ▇▇▇▇ ▇▇▇▇▇ who undertakes child care duties on my behalf.

I had been informed by Mrs Mc Darby and the ▇▇▇▇▇▇▇▇▇ social workers that Mary Manning's stepfather Sean Mc Darby had engaged in an ongoing sexual relationship with her and that he was the father of some if not all of her children.

I first spoke to Mary Manning, by phone call to the U.S.A. on 8 December 1987. I advised her to seek personal counselling in regard to her alleged sexual abuse. ▇▇▇▇▇▇▇▇▇▇▇ spoke to her by phone on 7 December 1987 and 28 January 1988 and gave her similar advice.

Mary Manning returned to Ireland in April 1988. I met her in person on 22 April 1988. She told me that she had an ongoing sexual relationship with her stepfather for about ten years from the age of 13 onwards. She did not describe the relationship in detail. She said that now she realised the exploitative nature of the relationship and wished it to end. She said that she never wished to see Sean Mc Darby again.

Subsequently, about October 1988, I discovered that Mary Manning continued to see Sean Mc Darby on a regular basis. On at least one occasion, when she came to Dundalk for an access visit to Ashley and Iseult, she arranged without the knowledge of the foster parents and social workers, for Sean Mc Darby to join her and the children for part of the visit.

On 6 December 1988, following an access visit to Ashley and Iseult, she had a detailed discussion with ▇▇▇▇▇▇▇▇▇▇▇ about her relationship with Sean Mc Darby. She said that her first sexual experience with him took place in the bathroom of her Ardee home. Her mother was drunk in a bedroom. She said that she could not confide in her mother because of her serious drink problem. She said that her relationship with Sean Mc Darby continued until she left her home in Mulhuddart in August 1987.

.../

Both ███████████ and I urged Mary Manning to undertake
counselling and therapy at the Rape Crisis Centre. She was
anxious to have Ashley and Iseult returned to her. Mary Manning,
in 1989, undertook extensive counselling under ███████ at
the Rape Crisis Centre. After discussions with ███████
██████████ and ███████████ and my own solicitor
███████ I agreed to return Ashley and Iseult to her in August
1989. Mary Manning had agreed to remain in counselling and
therapy and had undertaken not to allow Sean Mc Darby to have
access to the children.

Subsequently, we discovered that Mary Manning permitted Sean Mc
Darby to stay at her ███████ home from time to time and to see
the children on a regular basis.

███████████ and I met Sean Mc Darby and Mary Manning in
Dundalk on 29 May 1990 and 8 February 1991 to discuss revocation
of Fit Person Orders and on what conditions we might agree to
their revocation.

Sean Mc Darby acknowledged that he had a sexual relationship with
Mary Manning but he did not perceive it to be abusive.

Senior Social Worker